Y942.

The Year ROUND

THE YORKSHIRE POST
Story *of* Five Farms

The Year

ROUND

THE YORKSHIRE POST
Story *of* Five Farms

EDWARD HART

ALAN SUTTON PUBLISHING LIMITED

First published in the United Kingdom in 1994
Alan Sutton Publishing Limited
Phoenix Mill · Far Thrupp · Stroud · Gloucestershire

First published in the United States of America in 1994
Alan Sutton Publishing Inc.
83 Washington Street · Dover · NH 03820

British Library Cataloguing-in-Publication Data

A catalogue record for this book is available from the British Library.

ISBN 0–7509–0586–7

Cover Picture: Sheep at Low Fields Farm (photo by Ken Donald)

Library of Congress Cataloging-in-Publication Data applied for

Typeset in 11/14 Bembo.
Typesetting and origination by
Alan Sutton Publishing Limited.
Printed in Great Britain by
Redwood Books, Trowbridge.

CONTENTS

LIST OF ILLUSTRATIONS

ACKNOWLEDGEMENTS

The author and publisher are grateful to the following for permission to reproduce photographs:

Alan Barker, p. 134; Bob Benson of the *Yorkshire Post*, p. 110; the family of H.G. Clarke, p. 33; Ken and Betty Donald, pp. 28, 29, 51, 52, 55, 57, 60, 61, 62, 65, 66, 68, 70, 73, 77, 78, 81, 82; Eastern Air Views Ltd, p. 9; Audrey Hart, pp. 119, 121, 123, 127, 128, 130, 132, 133, 136; Harry Jones, p. 105; Massers of Malton, p. 2; Tony Sawyer, pp. 79, 80, 83; Virginia Scott, pp. 85, 86, 87, 92, 93, 96, 98, 101, 104; Des Stephens, pp. 4, 5, 6, 7, 8; Paul Stephens, pp. 16, 17, 20, 21; *Yorkshire Post*, pp. xii, 109, 118.

All other photographs are the property of the author.

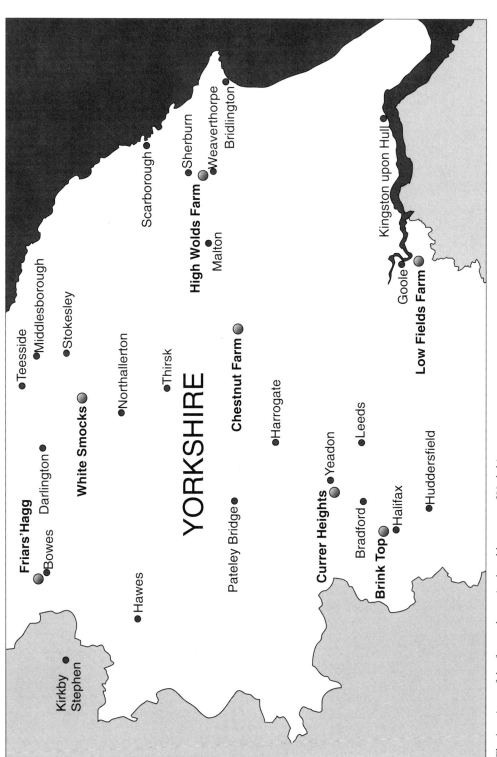

The locations of the farms, shown in the old county of Yorkshire.

INTRODUCTION

One sunny day in the spring of 1965, Derek Foster called to see me at Fair Hill Farm, Bilsdale, North Yorkshire, where I was both farmer and writer. His purpose was to ask me to help with a regular diary column in the *Yorkshire Post*, of which Derek was Agricultural Correspondent.

His idea was to describe the workings of four Yorkshire farms on a rota basis each Saturday. It was to be entitled 'The Year Round'. I was to find and contact suitable farmers, see if they would cooperate, and ensure that their diaries reached the *Yorkshire Post* on time. Lowland arable, producer-retailer dairy, Wolds cereals, and hill sheep were the suggested types.

As a farm feature writer for the northern and national Press, I had some likely farmers in mind, and sufficient contacts in the advisory world to ask for others.

Original recommendations have certainly borne fruit. For twenty-nine years 'The Year Round' has appeared each Saturday without a break, and until 1993 three of the five farms were the originals.

Chestnut Farm's contributions ended after ten years through the untimely death of Philip Ward, since when Low Fields Farm has maintained the flow. In 1968 Derek Foster suggested that an intensive livestock farm be brought in, and White Smocks has filled that role admirably ever since.

By then I was a full-time writer, and worked with Derek Foster on the project until his promotion to News Editor at the *Yorkshire Post*. Derek was awarded the OBE in 1989 for services to journalism. Fifteen years ago Robert Benson returned as *Yorkshire Post* Agricultural Correspondent, and he and Derek Hine deal with the weekly report when it reaches the Leeds office.

On leaving school I spent eight worthwhile and happy years as a farm worker gaining experience before starting on my own, and was always an avid reader. Yet in the scores of farm reports I read, nothing ever seemed to go wrong. 'I must have worked on some lousy farms!' I decided at the time. Yet all were well regarded locally, and some nationally. During a year as junior herdsman with Tom and Kathleen Hague at Dobcross, Oldham, I realized that my conclusions were wide of the mark. The Hagues' pedigree Ayrshire herd received a fair amount of Press coverage, but none of the mishaps and daily disasters was ever reported. There was no mention of cows going lame, of milking machines breaking down at crucial times, of calf scour, of disagreements among the staff, or nasty bulls.

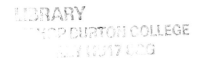

'The Year Round' gave me a chance to write about farming as it really happens. That aspect was stressed to the contributors, and all agreed not to skim over the disasters, but to report on damaged crops and admit to marketing decisions that turned out badly. So in 'The Year Round' lambs may die, cows milk disappointingly on second quality silage, corn come off the combine harvester far too wet, potatoes meet a poor trade, just as actually and regularly happens on even the best run farms.

The writing was to be in farmer's language, so that anyone with an interest in the land could understand it. Readers brought up on farms sometimes admit that they can no longer understand the technical features involving modern statistical management, and turn to 'The Year Round' where they can follow the farm's human story.

Not a few state that the column is the first they turn to each Saturday. These include farmers, advisers, technical representatives, retired farm workers and landowners. They can feel the ring of truth and share the disappointments of ill-got hay, the death of a good calf or a machinery breakdown at a vital stage, and the satisfactions of plans that work out well on the land.

EDWARD HART

'The Year Round's 21st birthday celebrations. This was the first time the group had met. Left to right: Dick Addison (Friars' Hagg); Edward Hart (writer); Paul Stephens (High Wolds Farm); Alan Barker (Low Fields Farm); Ken Donald (White Smocks); and Jim Scott (Currer Heights).

HIGH WOLDS FARM

Two of our farms are on top of the world – Friars' Hagg and High Wolds Farm. They are only 50 miles apart but in character entirely different. Whereas Friars' Hagg is a hill sheep farm, and cannot conceivably be anything else with its high rainfall and rough moorland grazings, High Wolds Farm is mainly arable. On the drier side of Britain with a 28 in average rainfall, it has large, well laid out fields.

Ironically, its true name is Moor Farm. Yet it was never heather moor; originally its land fell into what early nineteenth-century writers termed 'waste', or an uncultivated and undivided area outside the village and its strip systems. Unimproved grasses, shrubs and trees here and there, and a fair sprinkling of whin or gorse was the most likely covering at High Wolds Farm before it became an entity in itself.

That was in the 1860s, when an Enclosure Act – one of a series – enabled landowners to take in and fence land that had previously been common grazing for the villagers, a place where they could turn out their cattle and sheep, geese and pigs. These last made autumn use of beech mast and acorns – pannage – while there were also rights of turbary, i.e. peat or turf cutting for fuel.

Sledmere Estate and the Sykes family were instrumental in enclosing High Wolds Farm, building its homestead and laying out the fields on what had been termed Helperthorpe Moor. Sir Tatton Sykes was of that ilk, and the Druid in *Saddle and Sirloin* wrote: 'The reverence felt for him in Yorkshire was akin to idolatry. He rose with the lark and slashed his own hedges.'

There had been a chalk-built shelter on the site of the present farmstead, the chalk blocks held together with lime mortar. The chalk pit is still in evidence. On an Ordnance Survey map of 1856, High Wolds Farm is termed 'The Moor Barn'. The Estate was probably satisfied that the site of the old chalk building – in a slight declivity and with gently rising ground to west and south – could not be improved on, and so built the house and steading there. A feature of the Yorkshire Wolds is the siting of these steadings and the horseshoe-shaped shelterbelts that protect them from North Sea winds. The squires who hunted and shot over the open Wolds certainly knew what they were about. Bricks and tiles came from the new, so-called Weaverthorpe Station, which is in fact at Sherburn on the railway linking York, Malton and

Proximity to the North Sea makes the Yorkshire Wolds notorious for heavy and prolonged snows. The farm road has since been raised using the farm's own stone, enabling snow to blow clear more readily.

Scarborough. The station is 4 miles over a considerable hill from Weaverthorpe, and to reach High Wolds Farm with heavily-laden carts or waggons involved a long upward haul for the teams.

An arc of trees was planted to form a shelterbelt round the new steading. This lasted well over a century, which was just as well, for in the hard times from the 1880s to 1914, and through the desperate inter-war agricultural depression, there was no spare cash to invest except in immediate essentials. The shelterbelt is now being thinned and replanted, of which more later.

Maurice Fletcher, who still farms at nearby Sledmere, moved to High Wolds Farm with his father and mother in 1924. They followed Maurice's uncle, Maurice Garton, as tenants of the Sledmere Estate. The farm rent was 5s (25p) an acre. At one time eight horses were kept to work the farm's 309 acres, and when Maurice left school he and his father and brother were helped by two full-time men, with extras at harvest. The first tractor was bought in 1936.

Wolds farmers were indeed hard pressed in those days. A man's wage was 32s (£1.60) a week, and the two who lived in the farmhouse paid a small sum for their board. In the early days a lad would be paid only once a year, at Martinmass.

'The rate for a day's threshing was 7s (70p), and you carried on till the stack was finished,' said Maurice Fletcher. 'The attraction was a good dinner and two good 'lowances, as the mid-morning and mid-afternoon breaks were termed. There was a lot of unemployment in the villages, and men were glad to take a day's threshing.'

A change came in 1940, when Fred Ridley bought the farm's 309 acres for £2,900. A quarry owner, he had never seen High Wolds Farm when he bid for it. 'I thought it seemed cheap' was his reasoning.

During the Second World War, Russian, Italian and German prisoners helped on the farm. The only two disagreeable ones were from a U-boat crew, and worked for one day. During this period parts of the Wolds were given over to tank training in preparation for the Normandy landings. All sheep had to be sold off, and the tanks and Bren gun carriers had free range.

'My father and I had just finished stooking 14 acres in Long Field when some tanks appeared and flattened the lot,' Maurice Fletcher recalls. 'We got compensation of a sort, but it didn't repay the effort. Those were not very happy times. Troops were billeted in the farm buildings, and before the Normandy invasion were very quiet. They knew what was in store for them.'

After the 1947 winter, the Fletchers moved to their other farm at Garton, and in 1949 left High Wolds altogether. Their departure meant that High Wolds Farm could be sold with vacant possession. Des and Rene Stephens bought it for £18 an acre, borrowing money to do so at 4 per cent.

Rene Stephens came from a farming family; her father, 'Pop' Redhead, was a well-known East Riding character who emigrated to Canada in the 1920s, and contrived to marry and start a family there. He repeated the process when he returned to the Wolds.

Des Stephens had no farming background. He met Rene, a Manchester schoolteacher, when he was stationed at RAF Heaton Park during the Second World War, and they kept in touch. In 1947 they married, and Des found he had a lot of interest in his father-in-law's farm at Goodmanham near Market Weighton.

Hailing from a Herefordshire railway family, Des Stephens began to train as an accountant after his RAF days. He always maintained that this gave him an advantage in approaching farming with an open mind, and helped him break with tradition on several vital occasions.

Rene Stephens' father in those depressed inter-war years moved from one farm to another several times to obtain a lower rent. Some farms were let rent free, simply to keep them occupied. Most people farming during the two decades before 1939 remained haunted by them for the rest of their lives, and could never really believe that the new, comparative prosperity would last. It

Rene Stephens was part of the harvest team, a job she enjoyed.

was against this background that Des and Rene Stephens took over in 1949. High Wolds Farm was then 309 acres, and mainly under the plough. A proportion of short-term grass/clover leys contrasted with one field only recently reclaimed from whin bushes.

That first harvest in 1949's glorious summer totalled 163 tons. The wheat and spring barley averaged 1 ton per acre, the oats 15 cwt. Des Stephens was forcibly reminded of these early figures when in 1992 his son Paul phoned to say that they had combined 170 tons of corn in a day. 'More than our entire first harvest!' was his astonished father's response!

Nor were corn prices very high in those early years, hovering around £20 a ton. A flock of laying hens formed the backbone of the farm's economy. They were kept anywhere and everywhere; in deep litter houses, fold yards, or in huts about the fields.

For a number of years a flock of 200 breeding ewes was kept. They were big Suffolk–Scottish Halfbreds, strong enough to withstand the winter gales they faced while grazing on root crops on the big, exposed fields.

For a decade after 1949, Des Stephens farmed largely in the traditional Wolds manner, with cereals, sheep and leys. The first really big change in direction came in 1961. A broiler house for 12,000 birds was built. A

Pulling out of the yard at the end of Des Stephens' first threshing day in 1949.

The end result – corn in sacks leaving the farm. Craftsmanship of a high order is implicit in the immaculate way in which the sacks are stacked.

neighbour in the bungalow across the boundary asked, 'What on earth are you putting up?' 'That's only half of it,' Des Stephens replied. Today's capacity is over five times as much.

The farm still carried a laying flock, but profits had declined dramatically. The battery cage system which obviated the need for land was spreading, and specialist producers operating on a vast scale knocked out the mixed farm units. At High Wolds Farm the layers departed primarily through threat of disease carry-over from one broiler crop to the next.

'I wanted to start with broilers in 1959,' Des Stephens recalled. 'The bank manager saw my feasibility study and said NO. Then a year later he rang me to see if I was still interested. I said "Yes, but I need double the numbers to make up for the profits I've lost".' There is no doubt that the farm missed those early margins, considerable before broiler chickens were widely established.

That bank manager, in common with most people at the time, regarded chicken as a luxury meat for special occasions or perhaps weekends. It had certainly not then become a cheap form of protein in the human diet.

High Wolds Farm's first crop was housed in July 1961. After seventy-eight

Des Stephens was proud of his birds and of his straw yard system. The flock is healthy and happy.

days the average liveweight per bird was 3.88 lb, with 2.8 lb of meal needed to produce 1 lb of live chicken. Crops thirty years later reached the same weight in thirty-five days, at a feed conversion of only 2:1. Yet there is no more profit; the consumer benefits.

That original shed was purpose-built, and measured 240 ft × 40 ft. Over two million chickens have been reared in it. Another building 60 ft wide was built alongside in 1986, with a capacity to hold 24,000 birds. At the same time the first house was reconditioned and provided with extra fans, enabling it to take 16,000 birds. Total throughput thus became 40,000 birds four times a year.

The thinking behind this investment was to keep up margins in face of the ever narrowing profit per bird. With sheep and cattle gone, the broilers also created a balance between livestock and corn. Broiler manure has proved a factor in maintaining soil fertility and high cereal yields.

The farm's next big forward step came in 1964. Des Stephens visited the USA in the early 1960s, and there he saw bulk handling of grain for the first time. In Britain, tractors had replaced horses, first to haul the self-binders, and then the combine harvesters. Yet the end product, the corn, was still fed into big, heavy-duty railway sacks each holding 16 or 18 stone of wheat, 16 of barley or 12 stone of the lighter oats.

These bags were then slung across the shoulders of willing men who boasted they could 'carry sixteen stones up steps'. The steps led into the granary, sometimes ducking under low arches, and often through narrow doorways. The sacks were either set down to allow air round them, or their contents shot out onto the floor, to be shovelled into more sacks when sold later.

Des Stephens watched the American combine harvesters tip their contents into tankers or trailers drawn alongside. These were then driven to huge cylindrical grain stores into which the contents were augered without being touched by hand. No straining shoulders up narrow steps. Just the press of a switch, and the corn was moved automatically.

A line of silver storage bins was erected at High Wolds Farm in 1964. They were an innovation in the area. The National Agricultural Advisory Service (NAAS) staged open days and demonstrations, and many people came to look.

An early threshing day at High Wolds Farm. Total staff on the day would be at least nine or ten, including band cutter and feeder on the machine, two forking on the stack, straw carriers, corn carriers, and a lad carrying chaff.

The first bulk grain bins (top right), pictured in 1963 with the poultry yard (centre).

The bins incorporated a drier. Rainfall in the North American corn belts is generally far less than on the Wolds, where means of artificial drying are essential. Corn in sacks could be stored at up to 18 per cent moisture, air passing through the weave of the sacks sufficing to make it safe up to that percentage, quite high for an average harvest. Bins with their greater mass of grain were a different proposition. Their contents must be down to 15 per cent if stored for any length of time. Those six bins did almost thirty years' service.

Sheep figure frequently in the diaries for the first ten years. Des Stephens liked sheep, but had a constant battle against the late 1960s trend for specialization. In September 1969 he was being pressed to sell them, but followed his own judgement. That autumn he also increased the winter wheat acreage, a crop once seldom grown on the Wolds, but which was destined to become more and more important.

Most years, high winds during mid-September wreak havoc with standing corn on the Yorkshire Wolds. In 1969, however, most of the harvest was safely in store before conditions deteriorated and at High Wolds Farms the combine harvester finished its task on the 7th. With 375 acres of corn and a small staff, it is fairly typical of the chalk uplands of the county, which have lent themselves so readily to mechanization.

We finished harvest in August, but there have been far more years when we had not even started at this year's finishing date. Corn ripened far quicker than any of us would have dared forecast in those depressing months around seed time.

A week of very high humidity followed the last loads into the silo, so we were doubly thankful. Yields are not too bad, either. It is very noticeable that the earliest sown fields are the ones that yielded least, judging by the volume in the bins.

A 22 acre field of oats, the second corn crop after a two-year ley, yielded 55 tons. Spring wheat from 38 acres filled a 65 ton bin with acres left, and the final tally must be 85 tons. We hope for 35–6 cwt all round. Corn is weighing well, which is always a good indication. Our lorry drivers have instructions not to put more than 15 tons on a load, but though we do not fully fill them, they always seem to have more on.

Though harvest was extremely easy from the point of hard ground, standing crops and freedom from breakdowns, it was very tiring as there were no natural breaks weather-wise. Sultan is undoubtedly the barley of the year on the Wolds; none of ours was below 2 tons, but of course more than one year's experience is needed.

I was going out of sheep, but after this harvest have come to the conclusion that our system is OK. We apply broiler muck heavily to two-year leys grazed with sheep, and the results stand out even six years later. Our local NAAS chap had worked out a convincing budget which appeared to show that the sheep were not paying their way, but after walking round and seeing the crops which were after sheep, he said: 'Tear it up!'. Accordingly, I've bought another twenty-seven shearlings.

Most of the stubbles have already been dragged with our big cultivator. We plan to sow a much larger acreage of winter wheat than has been possible for many years. There is no doubt that it is the best money-spinner where it can be grown.

A month later he was pleased with lamb prices, and also described his methods of buying replacements at the autumn sales. His tail-piece was sound advice for buyers of any commodity anywhere. High Wolds Farm is but one arable holding where a strong plant is already showing in the drills.

It is twenty years since we grew winter wheat here, but 20 acres of grass grown for seed had to come out, also a 17 acre ley. Then we decided to sow 20 acres after spring wheat, and the weather remained so ideal that another spring wheat stubble was sown, making 77 acres in all.

This will cut down our spring work considerably, a big consideration as there is now only Doug and myself, together with our son, who has just left school. The variety of winter wheat chosen was Joss Cambier, a new one that has done exceptionally well.

Our biggest trouble was that the ground was actually too dry. We had to disc directly behind the plough to try and keep a bit of moisture. So far it has come up grand.

One friend on goodish land lower down could not drill in spring because it was too wet, and after a summer fallow it is too dry! He had to lay off drilling because it was coming up so unevenly.

We are not grumbling about the warm weather – it has been absolutely marvellous for getting on with jobs – but soil conditions have been very expensive on tractor tyres. However, it is a small price to pay; riding the drill has been pleasant compared with spring, when top coats didn't prevent one from being starved.

The lambs have all gone as stores, in two lots. At the second sale, they were just 10s a head up. We were ready for a good price, but it did not make up for lambing time losses; these increases never do fully recoup.

I did myself a good turn through buying twenty-seven shearlings as replacements early. At the bigger sales they would have cost more. I prefer to buy quietly at a small sale, after having had a good look round with plenty of time. At big events, people tend to get carried away, and live to regret it later.

In July 1976 the exceptionally dry summer caused shortage of grass. The lambs grazed close to the soil, picking up worm eggs that they would have missed in a 'grassy' year. Livestock people will all sympathise with Des Stephens' reaction of his 'heart in his boots'.

Corn on the Yorkshire Wolds was well established before the drought set in, and the season has been ideal for haymaking. At High Wolds Farm we cut 30 acres for hay, of which 22 were purposely set aside, and the rest closed up as we found that the sheep had plenty without them.

A Dutch bale accumulator was tried here this year. Towed behind the baler, it packs two rows of four, then releases them. Then five of these packs are set one on top of the other by bale lifter, and the forty bales led home by a squeezer bale transporter.

The problem of our old buildings remains. Hay has to be man-handled into them, so for this reason all fertilizer will be stored at the second farm, where the new 60 hp tractor and front loader stacks pallets of fertilizer, 35 cwt at a time. A trailer will be adapted or made to take three fertilizer pallets and one of corn – sufficent for 30 acres, or a day's drilling.

Hot weather creates problems among the poultry. Everyone wants to be rid of broilers at once, and when ours were due to go, the packers could accept only 3,200 out of the crop of 14,500. This relieved the situation, but to complicate matters during haytime, the cleaning hatch came off the bulk feed bin, and a ton of meal fell onto the roof. We had to retrieve it as best we could with the corn suction blower before the asbestos roof caved in.

The lambs caused more panic. They were drenched for worms so that they would need no more attention during haytime, but they began scouring badly. My heart was in my boots when I saw them; they had really taken a knock. A second dose cleared the trouble quickly, however, and it seems that the exceptional season has been the cause, and the type of drench was not to blame.

This metrication business is ridiculous. I notice that our feed firm planned to go metric, but has not done so. Fertilizer in 50 kilos is not too bad, approximating to 1 cwt, but I cannot see the farming fraternity falling for these senseless hectares. The unit is far too big, and if the Ministry wants returns in hectares, it can do the conversion themselves as far as I am concerned.

In August 1978 the sheep were still there, causing troubles inseparable from any livestock enterprise. Winter wheat was also proving unreliable at that altitude; new varieties and techniques have since improved the position.

Never before has combining begun in July at High Wolds Farm. By the end of the month we had harvested 80 acres, and have since continued at the rate of about 30 acres a day when fine.

Rains now don't do any good; they simply hold us up. Lack of rain when most needed is showing up only too clearly, for the early barley is very lean; it

lacked a good shower in late June to fill it. Though we have had worse stuff in the past, yields are well down on last year. These dry Wold soils are probably more affected by drought than any other northern holding featured weekly in 'The Year Round'.

A relative came to make up the harvest team. He looked after the corn pits while one of us combined, one ferried grain home and the third baled straw on the 'seeds'.

The six-year-old combine caused some trouble early on, and we vowed to have another before next harvest, but it has now settled down and may have won a reprieve.

Our 126 acres of Hassan barley have been harvested in the order sown, beginning with the late February drillings. We hope it will be good enough for malting, and merchants seem to be taking anything that is reasonably bold.

Winter wheat on the lower parts of the fields has done well, but on the ridges has died back rather than ripened. This is a common experience on the Wolds.

Feed prices for the next batch of broiler chicks are up £18 a ton, but we don't know what our prices for the birds will be. I don't see much future in the business.

Lambs have been weaned and dipped against fly, but will need to be dipped again to counter scab before sale. The main store sale is some weeks away, but two or three lambs may depart before then unless they alter their ways. They have learnt that the bottom strand of the electrified net is not live, and creep underneath it. They then rejoin their mums. Lambs are grazing foggs following the hay cut, and we are not too badly off for keep.

During the 1970s and '80s, mechanization proceeded apace. The Wolds farms with their big symmetrical fields proved ideal, and corn prices were high enough to service the investment. Des Stephens' son Paul was coming more and more into the picture, with the usual debates between the generations. But in May 1976 both were delighted with the new crop sprayer. Pressure of spring work is over at High Wolds Farm. Corn has been sprayed, and the next main tasks are sheep shearing and haytime. A high degree of mechanization accentuates differences between rush and slack periods, but enables jobs to be done when conditions are just right. The spraying machine with its 40 ft boom, covered 90 acres in one day, its 150 gallon tank holding enough for 10 acres.

I wonder if the other farms featured weekly in this column have had the same delayed response to nitrogen. Corn on the headland received twice the normal amount of nitrogen through double-drilling, and was a lot bigger than the rest of the field.

Crops on the hillsides looked a bit thin, but always tend to do so at this stage when one is looking into the field at an angle. We often get a bit worried in late May, feeling that things are not going to turn out as expected, but they usually recover.

The broiler crop is coming on nicely, and should gain another price rise before the birds go in a month's time.

Lambs need tidying up a bit, but will have to wait till we start clipping next week. We did manage to clean out the ewes' winter quarters, muck from the fold yard being heaped in a hill, as we term a midden on the Wolds.

Last summer we burnt stubbles after leading off the straw. I don't know if it is only coincidence, but two fields where we did not get a good burn are the only ones with any small rubbish, such as chickweed and charlock.

Some time ago in 'The Year Round' my father and I were debating whether to get a medium-sized 65 hp tractor in addition to our giant 106 hp and small models. New equipment has convinced us of the need, for a 30 cwt pallet on the fore-loader requires a fairly big tractor, as does bale handling. The latter can be dangerous if underpowered, and we wanted the quiet cab in any case.

Best crop here is winter wheat. This has been the case for some years, and leaf growth has been such that the drought did not penetrate. We shall watch the effect of expensive sprays on wild oats, our biggest corn worry these days.

By October, Paul seemed to have won the argument about the new tractor!

Winter wheat drilling is being completed at High Wolds Farm. We began 34 acres before the rains came, drilling twice round the headland before lunch after which I continued to drill non-stop, with our one man carting seed and fertilizer. The field was finished at 6 p.m., just two hours ahead of the rain which lasted a week. The remaining 28 acres had to await drier weather.

Wheat varieties are Flanders and Score, both new sorts. Seed for 62 acres totalled £1,000, the sort of cost that we are having to face, as are other northern farmers.

A four-furrow plough, bought for £50 last year, has made a marvellous job of the grasses. For stubbles we use the big six-furrow, and start that task in a week. It seemed a shame to plough in such a flush of grass after the sheep had been on short commons all summer, but we left till last the excellent growth following broiler manure, and crowded all the sheep onto it.

Stubbles on our 440 acres are very green with self-sown corn. This is general experience, caused not by rush or badly set combines, but by the high proportion of very light grains which simply flew to the back of the combine. They were not wanted in the sample, though all seem to grow. Also some corns died rather than ripened, and dropped to the ground at a touch instead of going through the harvester.

Our new 62 hp tractor is proving a grand asset. I wanted to buy one, but my father said we already had enough tractors. This model has been out every day since it came, and is so comfortable that the driver does not feel tired at night. Used with an ordinary muck bucket on the front, it loaded a 15 ton lorry with corn in 35 minutes, with help from a blower which probably accounted for 5 tons. We planned to have three 20 ton wagons in the yard at once, and borrow a neighbour's 1 ton bucket, but the loader broke down and we could not get all the transport together.

Store lambs averaged £15.50, with a top price of £21. We went mad and paid £120 for a very nice Suffolk tup to run with some newly bought shearlings. They have been tupped separately for February lambing.

Seven years later, in December 1983, a sprayer with double the boom width was acquired. Des Stephens had by then moved to Gloucestershire, and Paul and one man worked the farm. Scientific feeding went awry through no fault of the farmer.

We had a good look at Smithfield Show's machinery last week, without seeking anything in particular. Quite enough has been spent at High Wolds Farm this year.

Latest acquisition is a self-propelled sprayer with an 80 ft boom. Although second-hand, it is well equipped with a radar system to meter the spray and adjust the pressure to correspond with speed. The sprayer is built over a 68 hp tractor, and the tank sits where the cab would normally be, with the boom behind. In front is a new cab, so the operator has excellent visibility and control. The long boom is surprisingly stable, and one advantage is that so few passes are needed over a field that ground conditions matter less.

A rectangular 12 acre field was completed by going once round the headland and one turn across and back. The model was tried on patches of barley affected by mildew.

It seemed daft to spray in November, knowing that the first hard frost would check the disease, but the worst parts were worth doing.

Almost all the 1983 barley crop had been sold, but no wheat or oilseed rape. Bought-in feed for the broiler chicks caused problems. Our 15,000 birds suffered a bout of coccidiosis, rarely experienced these days as a control is added to the feed. It appears that the pre-mix element used by the

The first self-propelled sprayer, seen here in 1988.

compounders contained the wrong amount of medication, and as a result our birds lost so much weight that the feed company is compensating us.

In the mid-eighties the grass weed sterile brome was proving a problem. It is resistant to most sprays, and thrives in minimal cultivation regimes. Capital investment continued, vindicating the popular farmers' after-dinner joke, 'What would you do if you were left a million?' 'Continue to farm until I'd got through it!'

The last field of winter corn was drilled to schedule on 1 October at High Wolds Farm. All the corn went in very well, and germination is satisfactory. I had chance of a good look during spraying. That was my job, while our one employee dismantled an old wooden tractor shed.

A weed-killer against meadow grass has been used, for that weed builds up during continuous winter corn. Sterile brome is also controlled by the same spray, but as germination is over such a long period, at least two expensive sprays are needed.

It has taken me a year to get used to the sprayer's 80 ft boom. Tramlines or bare spaces between drillings are not used, but I count every eighth drill join, which gives the correct distance. A tankful of spray covers 25 acres, applied in

Spraying in Pit Field. The 80 ft (24 m) boom is angled from the cab's electro-hydraulic system at two points to follow contours, and the entire D-Mount sprayer drops off by pulling out four pins. Another computer measures acres and forward speed, and gives a constant rate of spray per acre.

Spraying in Pit Field during 1990 with the MB Trac.

an hour even when returning home to fill, so the machine enables us to wait till conditions are just right, and leaves few marks on the crop.

We have had one day's shooting, with a lot of game about and far too many hares. Old hands on the Wolds say that numbers are nothing to what they used to be, but hares seem to thrive on winter corn.

A 60 × 80 ft general purpose clear-span building is being erected. We keep buying machinery and have nowhere to put it, for today's models are too high for the old waggon sheds.

The farm's own chalk pit proved invaluable once more when this new implement shed was erected in 1984 and 1985. That winter was so cold that the men's gloves stuck to the steel girders. On the sloping site, costs below ground were very real, although hidden. February's diary was mainly concerned with this work, and tree planting.

Work is going ahead on a new shed at High Wolds Farm. The 80 ft × 60 ft frame is in place, block walls are being built and the roof sheeted.

The job is let out to contract, but my one assistant has led home 500 tons of stone from a farm chalk pit. He carried 7 tons a load and achieved thirty loads a day with help from a Drott loader. The site is now level, and will be concreted.

The other main job has been tree planting. Some hedgerow trees have been put in, and a conservation area of half an acre formed round an old dew pond.

A friend with a JCB digger cleaned out the 20 yd diameter pond – rather tentatively, as he didn't want to go through the clay, straw and stone bottom.

The pond is supposed to have been built by an old Wolds character, named 'Pondy' Welburn, who travelled the countryside with his horse and cart and had his own secret methods of dew pond construction. The horse was used to paddle in the stone on top of the clay and straw, and the idea was to condense moisture from the atmosphere.

We have planted bushes round the edges, and trees further back, making a much-needed feature from the house looking down the rather bare valley.

The home shelterbelt has also been interplanted with 2,500 trees, which will look nice in twenty years' time.

A nasty accident was narrowly avoided in the broiler house. I went for a routine last round-up at 11 p.m. to be met by a wall of heat. The regulator at the end of the house had failed, one heater had gone out and was leaking gas, while the other eleven were still burning. I turned off all supplies manually, so the firm concerned was not called out, though willing to come.

In January 1987 raising the half mile of straight farm road was reaping dividends.
February 1987 was hard, though not so desperate as the winter forty years previous.
Tonnages of feed stuffs needed were now far higher, particularly when the thousands of
broiler chickens had grown large frames with appetites to match.

A fresh lot of broiler chicks arrived at High Wolds Farm just before Christmas, and seems to have been our main concern. Half the 46,000 total were in the new house, only the second crop for this building. It has space heaters rather than brooders, and the baby chicks were kept in their batches by cardboard surrounds for the first crop. As they seemed to prefer tapping against this board instead of eating and drinking, it has been dispensed with, and lights down the centre attract the chicks to their food.

Our one employee returned from holiday last Monday, and has enrolled for an Agricultural Training Board combine harvester course. One is to be held here, so we have been tidying the shed in readiness. These courses are very good value for their small cost.

Last year we mentioned repairs to the farm road, using material from our own chalk pit. The old road had actually worn right through the original chalk, and had sunk well below field level. The result was water running for its full length and ending in the farmyard; by raising the level 2 ft, rain water now runs off sideways.

Grain leaving the farm in 25 ton loads necessitates a firm surface, as do big weights of broiler mash coming in. The trouble is that roads do not make any money; a few thousand pounds can soon be spent, for no return.

We had a difficult week during the snows at High Wolds Farm, supplying feed for the crop of 46,000 broiler chickens. We have storage for 30 tons, but as the birds grow they eat a 15 ton load in a few days.

After a struggle to bring the wagon to our farm road, I went out and bought a four-wheel-drive loading shovel. It will help pay for itself by operating under the Council's tender scheme, to open other roads in the area. Previously we had a two-wheel-drive forklift.

Intense frosts caused another broiler problem. With an outside temperature of minus 17 °C, against 22 to 25 °C indoors, condensation was far above average. This was particularly so in the old house, where insulation is less effective, resulting in wet walls and litter. It showed in the birds; pullets going at forty-two and forty-three days averaged 3.8 lb liveweight, but those in the new house were ¼ lb heavier.

Last harvest's feed wheat and biscuit wheat is being moved, and we are left with only the milling wheat to sell.

Late in 1988 came a most unwelcome blow. Publicity-seeking Edwina Currie MP linked the UK poultry flock with salmonella in a few careless words that did millions of pounds' worth of harm to the industry. Some specialist poultry keepers had to give up altogether; at High Wolds Farm there were fortunately other enterprises to keep the wheels turning. Faith in politicians, never high in the farming community, reached a new low.

This Edwina Currie egg business is absolutely sickening. At High Wolds Farm we have a broiler unit as well as 440 acres, mainly cereals, and wonder if there will be a knock-on effect on the chicken trade.

If 10 million hens are to be slaughtered, some will go onto the meat shelves and affect the price of our prime birds. Things are quite bad enough without that. Feed costs £25 a tonne more than a year ago, and we use 1,200 tonnes a year, while chick price is down 1p per pound. Soya, fishmeal and bean meal prices have dropped sharply and wheat remains constant, so why does the compound feed price not come down?

Our new crop of 45,000 birds ran into trouble straight away. I rejoiced when offered free sawdust from a local mill, which saved on purchased

MB Trac with four-furrow reversible 'vari-width' plough followed by a press to retain moisture. The plough is swung over at the ends and returns alongside the last furrow, obviating the need to set a ridge. With vari-width the furrow width can be adjusted from the seat. The scene is Near 36 Field, High Dale.

shavings. The birds have contracted the same spores that cause farmers' lung, and I've had to rethink.

Our land work is up to date. Our one man is doing the annual machinery maintenance round. I have been to a round of conferences, trying to find what the next five years hold for farmers, without much success.

My overriding impression is that Mrs Thatcher has lost all interest in farmers. The unfair Green pound remains; a German farmer said his milling wheat price is £40 per tonne above ours, or £100 an acre, and all because of the Green pound.

Paul Stephens knows from experience that oilseed rape yields are impossible to estimate from appearance of the crop. In August 1991 he was delighted to have some sheep and cattle back on the place; they grazed a dale, a common Wolds feature, where plateaux of level arable fields are bordered by steep dales. Unlike the Pennine dales, they seldom have running water. In the horse days these dales often provided summer pasturage.

In spite of the very dry May, we have not suffered too badly at High Wolds Farm. This chalk holds moisture better than limestone or sand and we had a good rain last week.

The New Holland TF 44 rotary combine, which has no straw walkers, cutting linseed in 1991.

Oilseed rape looks splendid, but I have been caught out before trying to estimate this crop. Financial prospects are certainly terrible, with a forecast price far below last year.

Oilseed rape keeps appearing in the wheat after two years. In the first year, seeds are presumably buried, and are then turned up again the next season. We have discovered that a shaft running through hollow compartments in an old seed drill has become worn and consequently some tiny oilseeds, which run everywhere, have escaped and been drilled in the next crop.

The grass weed sterile brome still occurs around the headlands but is not too serious.

For four nights I have been rising at 2 a.m. to help load broiler chickens. This crop has been difficult. Too much mortality occurred and the vets disagreed on the cause. I was pig-in-the-middle holding dead birds.

It is good to see some stock on the place again, as a friend rented four acres of re-seeded dale for sheep and cattle. Water, always the bugbear of these dry Wolds dales, is laid on and the stock is tucked away in a nice sheltered spot.

That summer saw the construction of another broiler house. Margins per bird grew ever tighter, and the extra numbers were an attempt to keep up profits.

In July the first crop of 30,000 birds was installed in the new house. These augment 42,000 in the two existing sheds.

The chicken job is in a bad way. We got no grants at all, yet a huge combine planning production of one million birds per week attracted a 15 per cent grant.

We smaller producers feel very bad about such a vast firm unbalancing the market. The giant plant is up for sale, and the sooner that happens or the thing closes down, the better for British family farmers trying to make a living.

Oilseed rape's flash of yellow has replaced the scarlet poppies that were a pre-1939 sight on the Wolds. Weed sprays cured the poppies, but accusations of farmers poisoning the land and wildlife with chemicals are badly aimed. Paul Stephens outlined his quandary in November 1991, and mentioned 'diversification schemes' now officially encouraged.

Oilseed rape at High Wolds Farm is still very, very small. It was fully a month late in germinating, and then had such a struggle to come through that it has lost its vigour. The plants are so minute that the pigeons can't see them! It's the one benefit as usually we are plagued by huge flocks.

I am also a bit jittery over the broiler crop. Pullets were sold at seven weeks, but the cockerels are being taken on to twelve weeks for Christmas dinners.

That means almost another three weeks of rapid growth with all the attendant risks. There are over 20,000 of these birds, which will weigh from 8 to 12 lb a piece when they finally go.

Wheats and barleys are nicely established, as are most crops on the Wolds.

All our cereals have been treated with weed-killer and aphicide, the latter to counter aphids which fly onto a crop and transmit the virus causing barley yellow dwarf virus. We would love to cut out this spray, but daren't. There is nothing to be seen until next June, when the affected crop yellows and dies.

With land work up to date my assistant has been cutting oil drums in half to sell for barbecues, and making silage feed barriers for a farmer friend.

Changing broiler chicken diets rather than relying on medication appeared successful in May 1993. Paul Stephens' views on set-aside accurately reflected the feelings of most British farmers, as did his remarks about farm legislation.

Varying the lighting pattern does seem to help the broiler chickens at High Wolds Farm. We have no precise results yet, as only the pullets in this batch of 65,000 birds have been sold. Cockerels are being kept to rather bigger weights.

The chickens also receive whole wheat among their finely-ground meal, which helps replace the grit they would pick up naturally. The result seems far more satisfactory than using so many injections and drugs which we are pressurized into buying.

At least that was my feeling after flying down to the Pig and Poultry Fair at the National Agricultural Centre, Warwickshire. From the air I could see every crop in every field and there are some very moderate ones. Set-aside is a Government mistake, as these surpluses of the 1980s vanish, and we could well have a shortage. I am ashamed of our own 60 acres of set-aside, with grass weeds, especially sterile brome, gone absolutely mad. They have no competition on the cultivated soil, but at least we can soon tackle them.

Winter corn on these 440 acres looks well and is receiving fertilizer, fungicide and weed-killer. March-sown oilseed rape is the worst, lacking vigour through delayed germination. Part of the trouble is a fuzzy seed-bed; I may have forgotten how to grow spring corn.

Every week brings new regulations which we must spend time in the office deciphering, instead of working on the land.

In June 1993 he reported a considerable capital investment, gearing up to try and meet whatever trading conditions the future held. He was still dispirited by set-aside.

Barleys at High Wolds Farm have already been laid by heavy rains. This entails uneven ripening and a poorer malting sample. Dry weather until harvest would suit me fine.

In typical farmer fashion I have left the long-overdue rebuilding of grain stores until the last minute. Present ones dating from 1961 can in no way meet forthcoming EC legislation requiring bird-proof and vermin-proof stores. A new concrete pad to last a lifetime is being laid by specialists.

Eight existing circular bins are being made into six bigger ones in two lines, with an overhead fixed conveyor replacing augers which needed two men to move them. Under the old drying method, hot air was blown up through the whole bin of stored grain. A new American system dries out 6 in at a time, automatically augered into the next bin when dry. Capital cost is high, and we are going ahead while we can afford it, so as to be geared up when harder arable times come in a few years.

Our one man has just delivered the last of the 1992 wheat, sold luckily before the price dropped.

The new crop of 65,000 broiler chicks has been installed. My wife and I and our man each carried four boxes of 100 chicks at a time, spacing them out over a house heated to 31 °C. A very warm job, but better than looking at the set-aside field, which is just a mess.

Construction of the new grain stores was still far from complete on 28 August. With such adverse publicity about uprooting hedgerows, farmers might be allowed credit when they plant for the future.

We are half-way through harvest at High Wolds Farm, and still without corn storage. Winter barley was sold off the field, and winter oilseed rape is being dried elsewhere.

Our new grain storage complex had an early July completion date. In spite of continued promises to send more men, the work is nowhere near complete. I became so desperate that when the construction firm's lorry arrived here en route for Scotland, I commandeered the ignition keys and said it was not moving until quicker progress was made. That worked.

Halcyon winter barley yielded a rather disappointing 48 cwt per acre, with variable malting quality. The crop was laid early on, and only one field of wheat is standing.

Broiler manure applied four years ago has only really worked this year, its effect presumably masked by three dry summers. We dress a quarter of the farm yearly, have the stuff analysed, and reduce artificial nitrogen accordingly, but consider a fresh approach.

A new crop of broilers is being installed, oilseed rape drilled, and some contracting done for neighbours.

The wood behind the house is being thinned, taking out larch and leaving the hardwoods, and making the place lighter already. The windward side is left unthinned for shelter. Five acres of steep dale are being planted with ash, beech, sycamore and cherry, and with shrubs like holly and field maple.

Early in 1994, more land was acquired. On this well-equipped farm, 440 acres proved insufficient for the farmer and one man to work economically, even allowing for a substantial broiler unit. When our story started between the wars, far more men were needed for half the acreage.

All winter-sown crops are being dressed with a low nitrogen compound at High Wolds Farm. Soil fertility in autumn was such that I decided against applying any fertilizer in the seed-bed, and during the wet winter much would have leached away. Plants are rather small and can feed on new dressings when they wake up, after which roots should penetrate to the fertility lower down.

Weed spraying is being done where necessary. Farmers are condemned for using weed sprays, yet cost keeps down any unnecessary use and prices are up another 3 to 5 per cent. When in the past I have tried to economize, I have regretted it a year or two later, when even stronger measures were needed.

A further 55 acres of arable land have been purchased. The block is 5 miles away, adjoining 110 acres that we contract-farm for another farmer. This all helps to spread overheads for our one man and the same combine harvester and other equipment will be able to cope.

These 55 new acres are all under oilseed rape. At first I regretted this but with an oilseed shortage in Europe it may turn out a bonus. That is if the wood pigeons leave any. There is a monster flock roaming the Wolds, turning 10 acres blue wherever they land.

The last crop of broiler chickens was rather disappointing. Present birds are doing better.

FRIARS' HAGG

Of all the farms featured in 'The Year Round', Friars' Hagg is the highest, and has the most inhospitable climate. It is part of the North Pennine chain, near the market town of Barnard Castle and the village of Bowes, and was on Yorkshire's western extremity until boundary changes lost it to Durham. From its high ground the Lake District fells may be seen to westward, while eastwards is the glow or pall of Teesside industry.

Yet this often stark and bleak countryside was among the first to be settled. There is a date stone at East Stoney Keld bearing the date 1664. Another date at Stoney Keld reads 1688, while Levy Pool nearer the moor and alongside Deepdale Beck has 1736 engraved on its stone. Its thatch lasted 196 years, and it is now a listed building, but 'renovation is fifty years too late,' say local families. 'If the houses were there at that time, I imagine that the fields were also,' said Dick Addison. Stoney Keld was his first home when he married Peggy in 1947. Their son Joseph, his wife, June, and family now live there, and their other son, John, and his wife, Hazel, and family are at East Stoney Keld. Dick and Peggy Addison moved to West Stoney Keld after buying it in 1984.

The 1,000 ft contour runs near East Stoney Keld farmhouse, and all the land is above that level. To the westward it rises to 1,600 ft near the Cumbrian border, and much of the moorland lies above 1,300 ft. On the uplands, every extra 100 ft means lower temperatures and later growth, and conditions are frequently harder than on many an Argyllshire holding of similar elevation.

When our story started, the Addisons had only 120 acres of meadow, and that with 200 acres of walled allotments had to provide hay and enclosures for Swaledale sheep grazing 2,000 acres of heather moorland. An 'allotment' in hill farming terms is an area, usually of just a few acres, that has its own stockproof boundary walls and may be used for holding ewes and lambs at lambingtime, ewes at tupping, or as an overnight stop for sheep brought down from the moor for clipping or drenching. It acts as a link between meadow and moor, but its rocks both above and below ground preclude any mechanical improvements of the sward. At Friars' Hagg the moor is only reached after a 3 mile trek along a farm track that the Addisons themselves maintain.

When I approached Teesdale accountant Sydney Addison to recommend suitable hill farms to write about, he suggested his brother at Stoney Keld,

Dick Addison (left) and Edward Hart discuss the forthcoming sheep sales.

Dick Addison.

stressing the relatively small amount of in-bye and the extreme difficulty of stocking high moorland at 3 miles distance from the steading and home pastures. Purchase of the intervening farm in 1984 ameliorated that difficulty.

From Ravock Castle near the farm's southern boundary on a clear day, mile after mile of hill unfolds and stretches to the Cumbrian border and beyond, with the Pennines' highest point, Mickle Fell, in view and often white in winter. The stone ruin of Ravock Castle stands on the Pennine Way, and an adjacent spring provided the water supply for Bowes Castle. Dryrigg Moss is just above it, altitude 1,245 ft. Over the boundary are Hare Moss, Hazelgill Rigg, Lancy Crags, and Battle Hill where the Dowson brothers also farm Swaledale sheep. Though he may not see them for weeks on end, Dick Addison is deeply appreciative of his good neighbours, for without them the hill man's life becomes impossible. On the best run farm, some sheep will stray, and the knowledge that any strays will always be returned at the first opportunity means much.

The hill farmer's job is to convert natural grasses and herbage into meat, wool and breeding stock. The sudden, disastrous storm that buries sheep in droves could wipe out overnight the progress of a decade, and hill farmers watch the weather as keenly and as continuously as any sailing ship's master.

Swaledale ewes and lambs at Friars' Hagg.

'To generalize about lowland farming is foolish; to generalize about hill farming is criminal,' said Lake District hill man George Wilson of Glencoyne. Friars' Hagg has its own peculiar problems, which include long stretches of heather with very little change in vegetation for the sheep. This 'black ground', as it is termed, does not grow sheep as quickly as a hill with heather interspersed with a range of natural grasses. Heather is a fine summer and early winter feed, but its growth hardly starts before June, and from March to May is the period of the hill ewe's greatest need. She is either carrying a lamb or trying to suckle it. On some moors, damp areas lead to the growth of the invaluable draw moss, a protein- and mineral-rich plant that shoots in late winter and is ideal for in-lamb ewes. Unfortunately, there are few such sites at Friars' Hagg.

Wet, windy weather is the sheep's biggest enemy, after heavy snows. The sheltering stone walls are far apart, and there is not a lot of broken ground to break the wind.

Besides the Swaledale sheep, grouse rank high in the upland economy. Sensible management usually ensures a sound breeding stock, and Friars' Hagg sheep break places in the deep snow where the birds can feed and shelter. Dick Addison has little sympathy with estate management elsewhere that drastically reduces the sheep stock in the mistaken belief that more feed will be left for the grouse. The reverse is often the case.

His sons do most of the daily winter foddering. John and Joseph each has a four-wheeled 'bike' with carrier for dogs and a small trailer loaded with bales of hay. Once hay feeding starts, it continues right through to the new growth that may appear with the first lambs.

These arrive on the allotments, each of a few acres, painstakingly won from the moor in days gone by. Twin lambs are brought in-bye, but only the shearlings lamb on the meadows. This is to allow them better grazing nearer home, where an eye can be kept on them in their first lambing. The drystone wall boundaries were erected using stone strewn on the fields themselves, and years of heavy stocking and manuring have made these meadows above the 1,000 ft contour highly productive.

Seldom does a hill farm enjoy better weather than the lowlands, but this happened in one early diary year, helping the sheep farming cycle to be restarted.

At Friars' Hagg we've been wonderfully lucky with the weather to date. When low lying areas were shrouded in fog, this high Pennine sheep farm was bathed in glorious sunshine.

Last Tuesday began equally bright, but by midday the fog arrived and made it two coats colder – quite miserable.

Fog is almost the last thing the hill sheep farmer wants at this season, for each day the ewes running with a particular ram have to be gathered round him from several score acres of moorland. In fog this work is obviously impossible, and some ewes may be missed. With one exception, all our rams have worked satisfactorily. They were turned to the ewes on 20 November and after one breeding cycle of seventeen days we know if the bulk are in lamb.

Bright colour marks on the ewes' rumps indicate a second mating. One older ram had too many ewes returning to service, and we replaced him. The others, including six new shearling rams, seem satisfactory.

Two of us set out shepherding every morning, and need a straight run with no complications over 3 miles of heather in order to be back for dinner time. A few sugar beet pulp nuts are being fed to counter the frosts.

There are full plenty grouse left for a sensible breeding stock, despite regular shooting. We wish readers well, but for the hill man a white Christmas should be nothing more than a light griming of snow.

Diaries from 1965 note a pleasing crop of kale for feeding lambs, and a reminder of the critically low prices then being obtained. The practical difficulties of carrying out correct veterinary procedures under extensive conditions are outlined.

Although all sheep have been dipped once this summer, we plan to dip again as there is some trouble from lice. A small body louse, similar to those found on cattle, has appeared. It is pink rather than blue, and other farmers have had similar infestations in their flocks. When one farming problem is overcome, another is sure to appear.

Kale sown Whit weekend is growing apace, a dark, even green, backed by 10 cwt of 15-8-8 compound in the seed-bed. Fodder radish is slightly

High summer in the 1960s. Mowing a heavy crop of grass with the 'little grey Fergie'.

disappointing to date, but this may be our fault for economizing with seed. At 6s per pound it is twice as dear as Giant Rape, and the seed is large, so 12 lb per acre hardly seemed sufficient for the conditions. Farm experiments lack the precision of officially conducted trials, and it is too early to give a definite opinion.

An acreage of greencrop at this season is vital to the hill man. In the drought of 1959, when keep everywhere was very scarce, the 'top' pen of forty from this large flock was bid to 49s (£2.45) and the next sixty to 30s (£1.50). Hill sheep farming cannot survive such prices, and the store market is so unpredictable that last year similar lambs topped £5.

Our greencrop is a buffer against glutted store markets, enabling us to finish lambs from November to New Year. Were no land available, some form of slatted yard would be considered, feeding bought barley and hay. The economics of this appear sound.

Single-suckled calves have had ample grass of late, and made good growth. Injections against blackleg are necessary here, and one year we lost a young calf born too late to be vaccinated with the rest of the herd. Those born out of season are now pricked soon after birth, while they can still be caught easily, though some suckler cows have temperaments which make this job unsafe to attempt single handed. Nor is it always easy to find the young calves, which may lie low for a week on the wildest stretches of the hill.

In 1971 tupping weather varied. The special problems of keeping the ewes with their appointed tups were outlined, relationships with game keepers mentioned, while the year ended with a grand day among fellow hill farmers at the Northumberland Experimental Husbandry Farm (EHF).

Autumn tupping season is almost as important to us as lambing time; severe storms are equally unwelcome now. Our first twelve tups were loosed in a mild spell, which quickly turned to real winter. Ewes soon start to lose condition in such circumstances, when for a heavy lamb crop it is essential that they at least hold their own.

We have tried a different system this year, with only two strong, well-tried rams on the moor, each with ninety ewes and well apart. In the past we had four, but dangers of mixing are considerable on an undivided stray, so we used our in-bye fields.

At home we have ten different lots. I usually shepherd these myself, and it takes a good part of the day to do properly. Some are 'chaser' tups loosed with just a small quantity of ewes, to make sure they are fertile.

A ram may become infertile between one year and another, and we deem this check worthwhile. The newly bought-in sires are all active, but we cannot tell their fertility until fourteen to seventeen days after first matings.

Rams are not changed until five weeks after turning out, or twice through the ewes' breeding cycle. They are then replaced with the chasers, but last year only seventeen lambed outside the five weeks.

We are busy with cattle and with lambs fattening inside. The latter are doing well, but need another week or so before the first draw. We brought them in earlier than usual in order to free the in-bye fields for the ewes.

A lot of grouse remain on the moor, but are now so wild that few more will be shot. One moor is keepered; the other we keeper ourselves, and help one another if need be.

Foxes are very quiet. If a covering of snow is followed by a few quiet days we shall be able to spot their footprints, often on a sheep track, for they are the same as people and like to travel easy.

A small party of us went to Redesdale EHF. We had a wonderful day, and appreciated the sensible way they are farming.

The first snows of the winter fell early in December 1971. Neighbouring sheep farmers living miles away by road were visited. Identification systems were explained.

Good neighbourliness is still found among hill sheep farmers, for without it, life would be wellnigh impossible. When we gather our Far Moor, which stretches right to the Westmorland border, we invariably find some stray sheep.

We have agreed among ourselves to deliver these to the rightful owner, for if we send a message, it means that someone has to wait about to help load them.

If there are only a few we take them of an evening, when time does not press so heavily, and so we hear the latest sheep world news.

These hill sheep are all identified by a system of colour marking, ear notching and horn burning. Seldom do we need to consult the Shepherds' Guide list, for we know all our neighbours' marks by heart, though they may live 20 miles away by road.

A fine September on the hills is a season to be relished, and 1972 brought such a time. Despite their bleakness, these moors harbour a whole range of bird life.

There is more than a touch of autumn in the air at Friars' Hagg. Earlier in the week some mild, soft days were followed by clear, hard nights with stars pricking out above the breeding stock of almost 1,000 Swaledales.

Hay is all tidied up. Some was spoilt through lying too long, but we finished with a record crop. One 13 acre field was grazed very late, and was left until all else was cleared. We were lucky; it was sweet, lovely hay, got without a drop of rain, and yielding 1,400 bales. About three-quarters of all our hay is very good, as we were more favoured than lowland farmers, fine weather coinciding with our later crops.

Heather was very backward until a month ago, since when it has come on really well. There has probably been a record bag of grouse on part of the moor, which is shot two or three times early, and then left. Occasionally we see black game, which are not as numerous here as some years ago. Besides snipe and curlew, the moor has any amount of small birds, especially larks.

Today is our local Bowes Show. A new cup for best Swaledale shearling ram cost £175, the most valuable cup in the neighbourhood that may be won outright. It is a real country show in every respect.

Cattle seldom feature in Friars' Hagg reports, though they contribute to the economy and help keep pastures in trim by grazing rough herbage. They must not interfere with sheep work. All seemed well in the April 1973 grouse-breeding season.

Winter struck Friars' Hagg with a vengeance immediately All Fools' Day had ended. Several inches of snow fell during the night, whipped deeper by fierce winds on a fellside whose lowest point is 1,300 ft. The Swaledale flock of almost 1,000 breeding ewes is in such good condition after weeks of mild weather that only a very severe turn for the worse would put lambing time in jeopardy, but nights like last Sunday are the very things we do not want when lambing starts in ten days' time.

We lost six out of over 600 fattening sheep; three through the feed and the rest through accidents, and this is as low a percentage as we can reasonably hope for.

All is quiet among the cattle, with a few to calve. We plan the minimum cattle work for April and May, when every minute is taken among sheep, once lambing starts.

We have been hornburning the gimmer hoggs retained for breeding. They also get two new colour marks, one denoting which of our two moors they are from, and the other showing to which section they belong. Numbered ear tags indicate both sire and dam.

Every year some fencing is replaced, and great progress was made in June 1973. Grouse were thriving, but at home an unwelcome intruder arrived.

Dry, pleasant June weather helps the whole year's work on a hill farm. This gap between lambing and shearing is used for maintenance and improvement, with tasks like fencing and road mending going ahead under ideal conditions for much of the month.

We replaced a mile of fencing on the moor last year, and are trying to do the same again. That length may even be exceeded, as my two sons and a neighbour erected eight nets in one day, or a quarter-mile. There is no difficulty driving posts; solid peat in the area more often means that cross-pieces must be nailed on to prevent the stobs sinking. A good stock of nets was on hand, but the next lot will cost 50 per cent more, £9 instead of £6. These are costs a farmer can do absolutely nothing about.

It will suit me fine if by next month's 'The Year Round' we have finished haymaking and shearing. Hill sheep farming alternates periods of intense activity – autumn sales, stock work throughout winter, lambing, shearing – with opportunities to catch up with jobs necessarily neglected.

We still have five late lambers, but long since stopped sitting up at nights with them! They are seen once a day, and take their luck for the rest of the time.

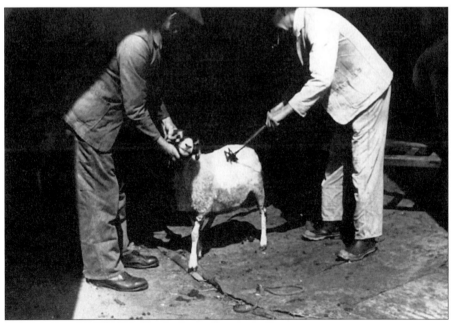

Clean and white after shearing, a Swaledale ewe is branded.

Young grouse are already on the wing. Neither they nor the old birds show up unless disturbed, and sometimes I find myself in among them, when they pop up on every side.

We had a fox around the buildings, which prompted me to mend my wife's henhouse door. She has some excellent goslings this year, which are now fairly safe.

In September 1973 Friars' Hagg still supplied young dairy cows. Dick Addison explained the marking system whereby records are kept of every individual sheep among many hundreds, and how the best families are retained.

There is always a demand for young cows reared on family farms on the dales. Buyers know that the animals have been quietly treated, and will fit into the more strenuous large herd routine with little trouble.

Friars' Hagg sells cows after their second or third calves. The last three have each topped the £180 mark, but younger cattle prices have eased to reflect farmers' uncertainties about costs and returns in the coming winter.

Dipping sheep is well underway. We wean the lambs at the same time, and now that all are ear-tagged and recorded, there is not the same necessity to keep them in their own lots. Each ewe's number is in a book with its lamb's number alongside. Some special families are kept for ram selection, and are known by our own names. One such strain we call John's Breed, originating from one good ewe my son picked years ago. Another is Gray Eye, from a foundation dam with very clear eyes, and a third is Red Bog, which merely indicates that the ground where that family runs is interspersed with ironstone springs.

The sporting season has gone fairly well. On one moor, as many birds were shot over dogs with no beaters, than on the other where butts and beaters drove the grouse in the now traditional way. We are always interested in the grouse/sheep balance, for many thousands of acres are managed for these two species.

In May 1974 lambing had gone well. It was still tremendously hard work and walking little lambs over the distances involved was inevitably time-consuming. But the end was in sight.

Lambing-time at Friars' Hagg is virtually over for another year. A grand time, with marvellous weather and only once have we had more twins. That was in 1960, following a very dry summer, and this year the ewes came to lamb in equally good form, travelling strongly although without a lot of flesh on their backs.

As work among them eases, we try to catch up with other jobs. Fertilizer is being spread on fields as soon as they are free of sheep, which go back to the hill with their lambs.

During lambing we began at 6 a.m., working longer and longer hours as the days lengthened. We like to be among the lambing ewes as long as it is light, but dare not start the last round too late in case of trouble. It is of no use timing it just half an hour before dusk, because if anything is amiss, darkness has fallen before we complete the round.

I look after the shearlings at Drovegill; they are always more prone to complications, this being their first lambing. One of my sons goes round the allotment sheep and the other does the cattle. I return for breakfast, deal with emergencies, and then we usually have lambs to mark.

We work among the strongest all the time, marking them and popping them into a separate field ready for the long drive to the moor. This needs four, so my wife helps. It is steady work; 2 miles is a long way for a lamb a few days old. Our enclosed fields are so limited that stock must be moved on at the earliest opportunity.

At last sheep are going out and no more are coming in, so stones and sticks are being cleared off the meadows and fertilizer applied. 'Get on and grow,' we say as we shut the gate.

The children join in too. A group of workers at the end of the day.

In June 1974 it was actually hotter than Friars' Hagg fencers appreciated! Clipping started and heather and stock looked well – far better than the economic climate.

Seldom is it too hot for comfortable work at 1,600 ft on the Pennines, but two such days occurred recently. A length of moorland fencing is renewed every year and cooler conditions were appreciated for the job.

Our contract for fat sheep has been renegotiated. Men in the trade are just as confused about future prospects as the rest of us. The position for all livestock is serious. Some barley-beef bullocks were withdrawn at £9 a cwt recently; at 8 cwt that is £72, and they probably cost most of it as calves.

In February 1974 Dick Addison discussed the pros and cons of storing hay on the moor in summer, against leading it out to the sheep in the sort of wild weather they had just experienced. He was not very thrilled with the economics of finishing store lambs on hill farms.

Winds, unpleasant on low ground, are desperately bad for man and beast at 1,600 ft. Heather holds hay off the sodden ground and prevents it from being blown away immediately, as happens on the smooth bent grass.

We are now making the 3 mile daily trek to the fell with a trailer load of hay. We have considered making a store nearer the sheep, but this is fraught with complications. If we ferried a big reserve there and had to bring the ewes home because of exceptional storms, we should be in a bad position. The sheds would need to be scattered over three or four strategic points on our 2,000 acres, and each must be substantial to withstand the weather. We should also have to build to keep mice at bay. We once filled a little shed on the moor with hay, and when we came to fodder it, every bale was nibbled loose by mice. I am not sure what type they are – black-looking little animals, more like a shrew.

Most of the fattening hoggs (last year's lambs) have gone to the butcher. They have thrived, probably 1 lb a head heavier than last year, averaging over 36 lb carcass weight. All were pure Swaledale, and included small gimmer or female lambs not retained for breeding.

The price per pound was near that for last year, but feed rose from £36 a ton to over £60, and would have topped £70 if I had not bought in advance. Profit on the venture is nil.

Barley is very dear when it reaches these hill places. My view is that there is an opening for the lowland man to set his stall out and buy quantities of hill lambs, run them on stubble or grass behind the cows, and add those extra pounds in weight more cheaply than we can.

Early March 1975 recorded more snow and the extra work entailed. There was an insight into the value of 'setting' dogs that point to sheep buried under drifts.

My two sons start for the moor directly after breakfast every morning, and on two occasions recently did not return until after dark. Though there was no great quantity of snow, it had filled the dips and a road had to be dug through for the tractors.

Frosts have been very severe, but we do not mind them, or bad weather in season. Our biggest hope is for some sensible, decent weather in March, so that ewes can reach the early-growing draw moss in addition to their hay ration.

During last week's snow we had nothing overblown, but three sheep were buried in the previous storm. The lads came across one with its head sticking out of a drift, and so found the others.

A good collie is useful for this. I believe that most collies can scent sheep below snow, but very few 'set' or point to them. That particular trait seems to be unconnected with other aptitudes, and regrettably we have none at the moment which can be relied on as a setter.

During a few days of light snow cover we saw fox tracks, but have not yet been lucky enough to catch up with the owner. Lambing time presents quite enough problems without fox losses.

A year later a severe storm could have caused a disaster, but most of May 1975 was kind.

Dawn till dusk is a literal description of work at Friars' Hagg in early May. Lambing almost 1,000 Swaledale breeding ewes began in mid-April, just after severe weather, during which the sheep ate as much hay as in dead of winter.

The most serious feature of the pre-lambing storm was its effect on grazing, which diminished daily just when the ewes most needed extra. Then on May Day we had a desperate amount of rain which set the open drains tearing down the hillsides.

Again, we lost no sheep, mainly because the weather was so severe that ewes and lambs were content to say in shelter, helped by full hay racks so that they had no need to forage in such conditions. Young lambs lay snug among the rushes, worth their place for this alone.

My sons went to the sheep at 6 a.m. each morning. I did the milking this year, then took over the shearlings from Joseph, who foddered the later lambers in a large walled allotment at the foot of the moor. John saw to the lambing ewes in other allotments nearer home.

Swaledale ewes and lambs above the 1,000 ft mark.

Everyone will not agree, but I'll be happy if we never have a worse lambing. One week was marvellous weather, so mild that no lambs born during the night took any harm. Nor have we had many difficult births. Old farmers say that there is a certain period of pregnancy during which mispresentations develop, should severe storms occur.

As soon as the moor was gathered and the ewes brought to their lambing quarters, we returned the gimmer hoggs (year-old females) to the fell. Right through winter the invaluable protein-rich draw moss was growing. Its growth is said to coincide with snowdrops in the garden, and the latter were killed by that mid-April storm.

In 1976 the drought was taking effect. By mid-August, all hill people were becoming worried that lowland farmers would have no keep and therefore be unable to buy their store lambs.

Friars' Hagg is becoming too dry. It is very, very seldom that we complain about drought here, but even the heather is beginning to crunch under foot, and it is not blossoming properly. Our sheep farm of more than 2,000 acres of moorland is cut by streams, so there is no shortage of water for stock, and we are not suffering as much as people on lower ground.

We secured good first cuts of hay, and are not too badly placed to meet the winter, but our worry is September and October, when store lambs should be leaving the farm in large numbers. Will there be buyers? Every sheep farmer is asking the same question, and with a high lambing percentage from almost 1,000 breeding Swaledales, we have a lot of mouths to feed.

Usually we wean the lambs about now, but this year they will stay on the moor with their dams until at least the end of the month. It is rather at the expense of the ewe, but we do what we can in the circumstances.

An extra load of straw has been bought. Straw can be used instead of hay for lambs finishing on barley, because if there is no rain and no store trade, that is what we must do.

I sent two cows to market, selling one and bringing the other home. She was a nice young Dales type of animal, and reached £190 when I expected another £60 or £70. It is a desperately difficult job trying to sell something that no one wants.

The best laid schemes can be set right back through accident, as in November 1976, when a missed sale opportunity added to the disappointment.

The first frosts have blackened the dahlias at Friars' Hagg, which is hardly surprising as the farm is at a height of 1,000 ft.

I was caught off-balance with the gimmer lambs. After such a good lambing, I expected everybody else to have plenty, and did not bother to prepare our surplus for sale. In the event I was wrong, and these ewe lambs were all back on the moor with their dams. We were very short of keep at home, and we could not fit in two or three spare days to gather them. They will have to go fat later, unless we find a private customer.

Our worst mishap was the loss in battle of a very good young tup. We brought all the tups down from the walled allotment to a secure pasture near home, and though they had been together all summer, they were upset with the change, and this animal was killed during the night or very early morning.

His stock are so clean, healthy and good that last month we bought his sire for £900 as a five-shear. The same sheep is grandsire of the record £4,400 tup sold at Kirkby Stephen in October.

The tribulations of farming on the hills were brought home in February 1977. Besides the immediate threat of lost or snow-covered sheep there was extra work in mending gaps in stone walls. Working collies are essential to hill sheep farmers, and Dick Addison grieved over the loss of a pup.

We've had rather too much snow for comfort at Friars' Hagg, but so far as we know, no sheep have been lost, though following that wicked Thursday night's storm there is one ewe we haven't accounted for. She may be among our neighbour's sheep, for with almost 1,000 breeding Swaledales ranging over 2,000 acres of moorland, we only have an exact count when the sheep are gathered for some particular purpose. One older sheep went off her legs, and was dead before we reached home with her over 3 miles of track, but that was not due directly to the storm.

Reaching the moor and foddering the sheep is a long morning's work for my two sons. Then there is little time left after attending to the gimmer hoggs at home, and extra jobs are all of the type that we may leave and return to later. We have tried to mend gaps on the moor walls as they occur, as they inevitably do when thaw follows hard frost and heavy snows.

The stock tups are in a field near home with a few older ewes that were not sent back to the moor. It is time they were parted; the tups are greedy feeders

Swaledale ewes and lambs in high stone wall country. The walls are subject to damage, particularly from snow and frost, and take scores of hours' maintenance each year.

and quite capable of knocking a heavily in-lamb ewe if they think she has some hay that they fancy.

Our feeding hoggs have nearly all gone and, despite the high price of corn, they managed to pay, although a fairly high autumn valuation was put on them.

We've had one sad accident. A grand little sheep dog pup being reared for work was housed in the cowshed. He always slept beside the bull, who would look at him and let him lie against his warm body. They were the best of friends, but one morning we found the pup dead, the bull having moved and laid on the pup's head. I was very grieved about this, for we are in a good position regarding dogs. Nap, Floss and Fan are all fully broken and can be taken to do any job on the moor with confidence, and we had looked forward to the youngster joining them.

The hill sheep's breeding cycle was clearly described in November 1983, when a big investment in an aged ram had borne fruit.

Last Monday the rams were turned with the ewes at Friars' Hagg. Allowing for Leap Year, this brings the start of lambing to our traditional date of 16 April when we hope there will be some growth on our high Pennine hills.

The breeding cycle for the Swaledale ewes is seventeen days and allowing the rams to run twice through, or thirty-four days, takes us to Christmas Eve. All ewes are then run into big lots, with 'chaser' rams to catch any still not in lamb, and our work eases considerably.

At present, each ram is in his individual field with a bunch of ewes varying from thirty to ninety. We had a hectic week selecting these and taking them to their various enclosures. Then the rams are taken out in tractor and trailer and each loosed with his allotted females. The ewes are gathered by our dogs to meet him and we always wait to see one sheep mated and know that the ram is working correctly. Generally this happens within a few minutes.

We take special interest in home-bred shearlings being used for the first time and in any bought-in sheep. One of our Swaledale rams is running for the ninth time. He was bought two years ago at Hawes for a high figure and has fulfilled our hopes. Two of his sons were sold and others are in use here.

May 1986 brought losses, sleepless nights and long hours. Yet imagine going out one morning to be met by thirty pairs of new twins!

These two were purchased at Hawes Swaledale ram sale. The sheep nearer the camera was seven-shear, and well proven, and cost £700 at that age. He had just the type of fleece the Addisons sought.

I can truthfully say that this is the hardest lambing we have ever known at Friars' Hagg. Lambing started on Wednesday 16 April on this high North Pennines farm, and on the previous Monday we gathered two lots of Swaledale ewes, each of several hundred head, from the far moors to walled allotments nearer home.

The weather was wicked. We plodged about in 6 in of snow and mist on the tops reaching to 1,600 ft, for even our lowest ground is around the 1,000 ft contour. On the Tuesday we could do nothing; rain came down in sheets. Some six ewes lambed early, but were mercifully alright. The problems came with the twins.

By Thursday we were lambing full blast, with forty sets of twins born, and the singles above that. Many shearlings, lambing for the first time, dropped twins, and after weeks of appalling weather had only milk for one. One lamb would have its stomach filled, while the other would be slower to start, causing 'bedtime headaches'.

On several nights one of my sons never got to bed. He fell asleep in his chair, and by the time he woke dawn was breaking. Four of us working outside were so overwhelmed that I engaged another competent local man. He began at 9 a.m. to feed lambs and help with problem cases, yet in the week clocked 112 hours! That shows how little sleep any of us had.

One night at darkening we had to bring in fourteen sets of newly-dropped twins. On another dawn we were met by thirty sets. In the end we had an enormous crop of lambs but more losses than normal. We can only say we did the best we could.

In September 1986 the hurricane that devastated so many fine trees further south wrought its own havoc in the hills.

Though the tail end of Hurricane Charley left its quota of damage at Friars' Hagg, things might have been worse. So far as we know we lost very few sheep, but cannot confirm until the autumn counts.

The beck that runs the length of this North Pennine farm rises near the fell end at 1,700 ft, continuing for 7 miles to the bottom boundary. For its first 2½ miles it runs unfenced through heather, but from then on is bounded by either wall or fence, pieces of which have disappeared.

We have not yet walked the full length, but walled allotments at the moor's edge are in a desperate mess. They are strewn with stones, while other walling stones were carried by the flood and lost altogether.

We have never seen so much water in summer, and it is debatable whether there was ever as much even in a thaw. Sheep dipping had to stop, but all the ewes and lambs are now dipped, and lambs speaned or weaned apart from seven baby lambs, not born until July or even August.

Living on top of the world usually allows warning of storm, as in November 1986. It was back to the solitude of the open moors and damp fields after the bustle and good company of the sales.

On wild November afternoons we could see the bad weather coming in waves at Friars' Hagg.

Our main job this week has been gathering the Swaledale ewes from the various sections of the moor, and clipping tails ready for tupping. We take a strip of wool off either side of the tail, so that the ram is not impeded. Shepherds on lower ground clip the inner thigh as well, but we leave as much wool as possible for winter protection.

All the excitement of the ram sales is over once more. We had a good 'tup trade', ending with a credit balance against purchases – unusual for us.

We bought five Swaledale shearling rams, having planned only four; one we set our hearts on was sold very late on the final day, so if we missed him there was nothing left. Our bid was successful, but meanwhile we had bought another at less money.

To return to the moors, the only decent show of grouse is where the birds fed among the sheep in last winter's storms.

January 1987 produced some violent storms. When dales farmers can't reach their sheep, things are pretty bad. But few people appreciate good food and a comfortable house more!

We don't want too many days at Friars' Hagg like last Wednesday week. It was one of those days the hill sheep farmer really dreads: snowing and blowing heavens high throughout. We couldn't see more than a few yards and even then we were choked by flying snow.

One lot of sheep we didn't reach; it was too dangerous. Nor was it any good thinking that we could turn round and safely retrace our steps, because a few moments later they weren't there. However, these particular Swaledale ewes had been well foddered the day before; we knew where we had them, among some long heather. We fed them again early the next morning and they had taken no harm.

Sheep from the other lots had been brought nearer home, some being fed twice daily. We finish early morning work around the buildings so we can be away to the sheep at daybreak, which makes a tiring day, though nothing like as long as in lambing time or haytime.

The trouble is that as soon as we come in to a warm fire after all day in the bitter cold, we fall asleep!

There's always something new in livestock breeding, and Dick Addison puzzled over lambs being born well after the normal gestation period. Yet 1987 proved far easier than its predecessor.

Lambing time conditions at Friars' Hagg have been too good to complain about. There is just no comparison with last year's vile weather and, though the crop is not quite as heavy, lambs seem healthy and good.

We have also been wonderfully lucky in the small number of difficult births. Other shepherds speak of 'hung' lambs partly delivered and unable to make the final push. On hill sheep farms like this extensive north Pennines holding, it is impossible to see sheep more than two or three times a day.

One odd occurrence is the number of lambs coming late. We know from the colour markings left by the rams that a high proportion is three or four days beyond the recognized time, presumably due to the season.

It's busy, tiring work, but when we think back to last year's constant wet and cold and the nights we never got to bed, we wonder how we got through.

In June 1987 the skills and effort involved in moving ewes with young lambs were highlighted, for every lamb must be reunited with its mum at the end of the drive, or it might never find her.

Swaledale ewes with single lambs go back to their respective moors as soon as they are strong enough. Last week we took a batch of 150 ewes on a 2½ mile trek, crossing a stream en route. This is a full day's work. First, all the sheep on a 90 acre allotment are gathered, and those with the appropriate fleece mark for the particular moor are run off.

We cannot use pens or drafting races, as we must check that every ewe has her lamb with her. Three or four men, each with a dog, are needed, and six or eight couples may present themselves in front of the flock and be allowed to run off. Then a ewe appears with no lamb, stopping the whole process.

Those destined for another moor, or with lambs too small to travel, are turned the other way. Sometimes the 'shed' is completed in an hour, or may take twice as long. The drive, including crossing the stream, takes three hours when lambs are young. Then, when the moor is reached, we have to couple them up all over again, after the hassle of the journey. Then we walk home.

February 1988 proved tough, but a new mechanical acquisition helped the battle against distance and the snows.

Early winter weather has been very bad for stock. We take extra fodder daily to our large number of Swaledale ewes to try and partly compensate for the atrocious conditions. Winds have been such that the sheep cannot lie. They are driven by the wind into shelter which is naturally wetter, and now paddled by constant use.

A new acquisition this year is a four-wheeled motorized bike with a little trailer behind. We set off with two trailers and the bike, carrying fodder for six lots of sheep, feeding them at widely separated points so that they spread out over the whole moor and graze more evenly.

The first tractor feeds two lots, and the bike is loaded from it and fodders another lot further out. Then it crosses over and meets the second tractor and again fodders an outlying bunch of sheep, possibly 5 miles from home.

The 1988 sales painted a brighter picture, but John and Joseph's Mule breeding ideas did not really pay off.

We have been sorting and selling ewes and lambs. Our surplus Swaledale gimmer lambs pleased us very well, one draw of forty averaging just £60, and a larger batch almost as much. That is after drawing out the best females for our own stock.

Last autumn, I reported that my sons were so taken with the Mule ewe lamb trade that they tried a Bluefaced Leicester tup on Swaledales not good enough for pure breeding. I now admit that the resulting Mule ewe lambs averaged a few coppers less than the pure Swales!

Our draft Swaledale ewes sold for further breeding on lower ground more sheltered than these moors ranging to 1,600 ft to average £70. We are now starting among the wether lambs, sorting to suit the grader.

Then come the ram sales, the peak of the year. Even though there is no outstanding sheep, we have a packet of big, reachy, good coloured stock tups, of the mould that people want their ewes to look like.

Prices cannot be forecast; it just depends on who wants them. Two men intent on the same animal can send bids far beyond our expectation; conversely, a sheep that we think a great deal about may be under-priced.

'Quiet snow' in February 1992 wreaked havoc in lowland cities, but was no problem to hill farmers, who took it in their stride.

Muck and maintenance sums up work at Friars' Hagg in February's first half. The weather was grand till we had a fall of snow early this week, but it was a quiet snow with no wind and therefore no problems.

Manure from the cattle sheds was led out in fine weather and there was the never-ending task of keeping up the drystone walls. It's no use having planned matings if you can't guarantee that the sheep will stop in the field where you left them.

Our farthest boundary is 7 miles from home over rough tracks. One of our two sons who fodders the sheep up there reported that he had been within 150 yd of the boundary almost at the 1,600 ft contour.

If the weather is sensible, this hay is fed where the sheep are, encouraging them to range widely. If snow threatens they will probably come down on their own. Mickle Fell and Crossfell, a few miles away, have been white-capped for some time.

The Swaledale stock tups winter in meadow fields near the house in three lots. Shearlings, elder tups and the prime middle-aged sheep each have their own group.

In 1992 lambing got off to another difficult start but with the thrill of finding some exceptionally good lambs, the result of generations of careful breeding. Dick Addison once said: 'If we hadn't something good to look at, we would never stick it'. The last thing they wanted was a bad-tempered newly-calven cow. . . .

Lambing at Friars' Hagg began with two dreadful April days. Rain, sleet and snow are not much fun for newborn lambs above the 1,000 ft contour. Fortunately, few ewes lambed on those days, and with the ground so sodden any dry days are welcome.

Our two sons and I lamb this large stock of Swaledales, with one man on other work. We managed wonderfully with two part-time lambers but one

Dick Addison (left) and Edward Hart with the home-designed cattle feeder, mobile and of waste-free pattern.

Limousin-cross cows and calves enjoy the August sun at Friars' Hagg.

unfortunately had his leg broken by a cow at home, so we have help only every other day.

I look after all the shearlings lambing for the first time on one moor, and the ewes on another. Everyone has his own patch, and we are so busy that some days we never see one another. On Tuesday we marked a packet of eighty lambs from which five or six might make stock tups. Twins have been fewer so far.

The spring birds have returned to these high moors near the Cumbrian border. I saw two golden plovers, with any amount of curlews. The grouse are very quiet, a good sign indicating that they are nesting tight.

One awkward cow is adding to our work. She is protective with her calf, but just didn't get to suck right. The mother is so nasty with her head that it takes two men and a gate to make her suckle her offspring.

October 1993 was among the wettest on record, to be followed by an equally unpleasant November, but sale dates could not wait for dry days.

Continuous downpours at Friars' Hagg have saturated the hills and made outdoor jobs unpleasant. Although some tasks are done undercover, there will be no let-up here until mid-November.

We have to meet several sale deadlines each week. It is common practice to dip all sale sheep to give that little extra colour to their fleeces, and once the dip has dried on them it will withstand rain.

No such fine day occurred and we took the risk on a showery one, but we might as well have been backing horses. The heavens opened soon after the last sheep was through, and washed the dip from the fleeces. It was a complete waste of time and dip.

We have sold our surplus Swaledale ewe lambs at prices nicely above last year.

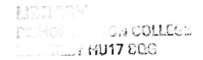

WHITE SMOCKS

In 1959 Ken Donald left home to marry Betty and take on White Smocks. He had worked for his father on a rented farm at Hutton Bonville, on the other side of Northallerton, North Yorkshire. As was not uncommon at the time, Ken received his board but no wages; any extra income came from pigs fattened in buildings otherwise empty during summer.

Ken Donald left school at fifteen. His grandfather had been a railwayman at Bowes, near Barnard Castle, and his father began as a farm servant before starting on his own. Always good with his hands, Ken Donald had done much to improve buildings and facilities on his father's rented farm. But at the end of the day it was not theirs. He determined to own his own place, however small.

The chance came through White Smocks and its 37 acres. Ken Donald had saved £800, and that was all the money he had. He and Betty borrowed every

A view of the bungalow and steading, taken from a neighbour's field in 1993. Every year a photograph of White Smocks' buildings is likely to show additions and alterations!

penny of the £4,800 purchase price. 'Had we known how things would go, we should have bought a bigger place,' he said. 'At the time, farming was rather stagnant. Not until the mid-1960s did grants improve, and every encouragement given to increase production. Then EC grants gave further stimulus.'

Ken Donald knew what he wanted. Something cheap, with scope to improve and build up. He certainly found it at White Smocks, its dilapidated house and few brick buildings standing pleasantly – its real name is Mount Pleasant – on a low rise, its soil a potentially fertile but fairly heavy loam.

The farm was on a plain sheltered by the Cleveland Hills to the south-east. To make the most of the acreage and give a rapid turnover, pigs and poultry became the main lines. Had Ken Donald bought more acres at the time, he would probably not have figured in 'The Year Round', for an intensive livestock holding was sought by the *Yorkshire Post* to balance the larger scale arable, dairying and hill sheep enterprises.

Ken and Betty Donald embarked on their own, working hard and long, always reinvesting and improving. Those were inflationary times. One of Ken's maxims is 'Only those with something to inflate can benefit from inflation', and he followed that precept for the next thirty years.

An adjoining 8 acre field was purchased, bringing the total to 45. In March 1969 Ken Donald was once again all set to start an improvement that would either enable work to be done more quickly or extra stock to be kept. Sheep, which were to become a regular feature, were mentioned by June 1969.

This was the situation as I found it in December 1968, as reported in the Yorkshire Post.

Intensification of housed stock, rather than more acres, is the aim of Mr Kenneth Donald, Mount Pleasant Farm, West Rounton, Northallerton. He has 45 acres, 40 breeding pigs, 3,000 layers – and 100 sheep.

He buys his milk, and his fields are useful for taking the increased quantities of manure from pigs and poultry, and are dressed every three years. Potatoes provide a welcome cash crop, while heavy crops of oats and barley are home-fed and yield straw for litter.

Though Mr Donald left a much larger family farm nine years ago, he is quite satisfied that he has sufficient scope for expansion. He and his one man, Len Horton, are able to carry out many extensions themselves to the compact range of buildings.

A current project is the levelling of brick rubble, so that lorries may reach the laying houses direct, via a concrete road, and one feels that Mount

A fine litter in the farrowing quarters.

Pleasant's owners hurry the completion of each new venture so that they can press on with the next.

Pride of place so far goes to two farrowing houses, accommodating fifteen sows. The pens are of an original design and though Mr Donald gained some ideas from the farming press, the essential details are his own.

Each sty is 8 sq ft, backed by a dung passage 4 ft 6 in wide. Gates across the passage swing in to close this area off from the pen when farrowing takes place, so that piglets do not stray.

Another gate is swung from the front of the pen to form a farrowing crate when in one position, a creep for the piglets when in another. Parallel to it, when in crate position, are three horizontal bars forming a creep on the other side, so that youngsters are safe whichever way the sow lies.

One drawback to the present arrangement is that all cleaning out has to be done manually. Up to about a month old, this is a comparatively simple matter, but thereafter, Mr Donald feels that mechanized cleaning would be well worthwhile for older piglets.

He is, therefore, planning another building, with scraper cleaning, which will take two sows with their litters from that stage. At present, dung is removed twice a week.

Foundation stock were Large Whites. These were crossed with Landrace boars, and the progeny bred back to Large Whites. Recent offspring have been put to a good Landrace boar, so that Mr Donald has in effect his own strain of Large White/Landrace.

Results have been consistently good, and under the Pig Industry Development Association's (PIDA) recording scheme, show that 10.1 pigs are reared per litter, from 11.3 born alive. Each sow averaged 1.9 litters per year.

Total feed cost per pig weaned, was £3 9s 10d. Figures for food consumption per pound of weaner produced were exceptionally good, 3.6 lb against a national standard of good, 5; average, 6.5. Feed costs per pound of weaner produced were also outstanding, 1.2 against PIDA's average of 2.2.

Mr Donald found that coloured ear tags were frequently lost from sows' ears, and he has reverted to the old system of notching. Differently positioned notches for 1, 2, 3, and 5 give any combination up to 10, in the near ear, while similar notches in the far ear are used for 10s. Thus the sow may be given any number up to 100.

An interesting feature of the farrowing houses is a large blackboard columned to show each sow's performance and stage. Her number is followed by date served, then three weeks date, date due and date farrowed followed by deaths, eight weeks date and number of piglets at eight weeks.

Age sold and total litter weight in pounds is also recorded, with any general remarks.

'Before we started this recording system, we used to write these dates down on any old bit of paper. Len had some and I had some, and we never knew where we were. Now we can see at a glance the progress of any sow, although each has an individual record sheet in book form.'

Weaners are sold on contract to a private buyer, on a liveweight basis, and reach 60 lb in about ten weeks.

Poultry were the main line, but are being kept at present strength of 3,000 broiler breeders. These arrive as day-olds, in two 1,500 batches. They are Arbor Acres, and come into lay at 23–4 weeks.

Of a meat type, they have not the laying persistency of the commercial egg producer, but lay up to 80 per cent with peak average of 75–6 per cent. This declines steadily after six weeks in lay, until they are uneconomic. Then they are sold, after about eight months in lay. Hatchability is very good, approaching 90 per cent.

The flock is housed on deep litter, with bulk hoppers and automatic watering, so that egg collection and grading are the only routine jobs. Mrs Donald is responsible for much of this.

Other stock are ninety lambs, some of which may be finished inside, and fourteen Masham ewes. Of twenty-four tupped last autumn, one died, six had singles and the rest doubles. Thus they play a useful if small part on a small farm with a big turnover.

Sheltered at the foot of the Cleveland Hills, White Smocks was affected less by the blizzards than many larger farms in March 1969 because the bulk of its winter work is under cover anyway. But in a storm, all jobs take longer, and tending stock filled most of the days.

We took advantage of the mild January to bring our hedging up to date, going round with a small power machine attached to the tractor.

It is quite suitable for one- or two-year-old growth, and a lot faster than slashing by hand. There is just half a day's work left, and then we shall have got round the lot – for the first time since I came here.

Although everything is laid out to start a concreting job, the actual laying has not begun. It is difficult to fit in, as hard frosts must be avoided, and when spring comes we shall be too busy with other things. The area concerned is an apron in front of a store shed, and has been approved for Farm Improvement grant. Its 85 sq yd will join up with other hard surfaces. We have already laid

Broiler breeders feeding (foreground) and perching.

200 land tiles to lead the water away, as it was a very bad place for standing water.

The laying birds producing eggs for broiler breeding are doing very well. They did drop slightly during the very frosty weather, as in spite of controlled environment housing it is difficult to keep temperature up to the 58 °F that we should like. Fans are set on interval timing to run one minute in ten, just to change the air.

Besides these 3,000 birds we have a herd of forty sows producing strong weaners for sale by contract. One gilt reared eleven, which at nine weeks averaged 49 lb liveweight, while two sows had twenty-one between them which averaged 58 lb at sixty-six days.

If we could keep up those sort of figures we should be all right, and naturally we aim in that direction by keeping breeding gilts from the best families.

I always draw out four or five more than are needed, so that some may be culled; it also allows for those not in-pig. From the last twelve retained, only seven are now in the herd.

Our old boar has had to go. He did a good job, and his successor has sired 112 live piglets in eleven litters from gilts, so is proven in that direction.

Our only other stock are sheep, and besides a small breeding flock we have

Willing helpers at the potato riddle. Very heavy slurry dressings produce big crops at White Smocks.

sixty hoggs to be run on, clipped, and fattened off grass. I think this will pay better than trying to fatten them outside on bought feed.

In June of that year, the potato crop made news. One field of about 7 acres was usually cropped with potatoes in rotation every year and, while the acreage was small and the equipment primitive, the crop had one great virtue. It was especially valuable to make use of the vast quantities of slurry and poultry manure that had to go somewhere. That somewhere always included a stubble destined for potatoes, and the resulting crops of around 20 tons per acre compared well with specialists on much better potato land. The one hot week early in the month was a real saving grace for White Smocks, as for other northern farms.

I had hoped to attend a beef-from-grass-and-barley demonstration on a nearby farm, but the day was sunny and we were planting potatoes, of all jobs. Never before have we been anything like as late, although on one occasion it was the last week in May before seed arrived for the last acre. They did very well; the soil was warm and they never looked back.

It seems that twelve to fourteen weeks' growth is plenty for the crop. On

Tractor driver's view of potato riddling.

dry soils early sowing may be all right, but on other types it seems to have got out of hand. Some early-sown corn round here looks very yellow, but in a season like this it's a job to know what to do.

Little is happening on the poultry front. The batch of layers is performing normally, with the expected 2–3 per cent drop in production weekly. Considering rearing setbacks, they are satisfactory. One house is being rested at the moment, and the other will be given a two months' break, so the next lot should start with a clean sheet.

From six sows farrowing in June, three are rearing eleven apiece and three have ten, so that's not too bad. There are eleven due in July – I had a count on Monday – thus the cleaned and disinfected accommodation we were working on last time should come in handy.

Plans are also afoot to convert two loose boxes into five farrowing pens; we shall clear the boxes ourselves, then the local builder takes over.

Another building job is blocking round the Dutch barn, using hollow concrete blocks. Used chiefly for hay and potato storage, it may also serve for calves if an idea for contract rearing materializes.

On a 6 acre grass we have thirteen ewes with twenty-two lambs, and seventeen hoggs retained from last year. The sheep have paid, but we are too restricted in acreage to give them a change, and I think the best way is to wear out the ewes and rest the whole farm for a year or two. Then we can start up again on clean land.

In September 1970 Ken Donald recorded a time when 'everything in the garden is lovely'. Farmers do well to rejoice on such occasions; they never last for long. A combination of wind and sun enabled some bonus hay to be made, and carefully thought-out breeding plans in the pig herd were going according to plan. 'A man makes only one really good second crop of hay in his lifetime' is a Yorkshire saying, but that year farmers were lucky with the weather for late hay.

Our 7 acres of second-crop clover was opened out with the mower a fortnight ago, just in time to catch some heavy rain. The rest of the field was cut in better weather, and lay for just a week before we got it in very nice condition.

The day it was baled was every farmer's dream of ideal harvest weather; strong sunshine and a stiff breeze. It was so windy that we had to row the hay up and down wind in front of the baler, for if we went round and round the windrows were simply blown into one another at the ends.

I estimate this second hay crop at 25–30 cwt per acre. It follows a first cut

which was sold from the field at just over 3 tons an acre, so there was no guesswork about that.

Fortunately, things have been fairly quiet among the pigs. Three gilts have farrowed, out of a batch of eleven. Farrowing dates for this lot have got a bit scattered, I'm afraid. We did better with four sows, which were weaned together, and all came on heat together.

Two were served by our old boar, and two by AI (artificial insemination). This AI service is a remarkably economic way of getting blood from a boar rated at 160 or 170 points, which is very high; the aristocracy of the pig world, in fact. It must be a sound way of herd improvement.

One of the few visits I have made recently was to a Meat and Livestock Commission (MLC) farm walk. The pig farm concerned has sixty sows, and used AI throughout.

Our first broiler crop is five weeks old. They seem to be doing well to date. Mortality has been higher than we should have liked, but our advisers think that results will be satisfactory if the birds continue to grow as quickly as they are doing.

By July, 1971 was proving an exceptional 'grow year', with associated problems of dealing with the surplus. Not content with improvements to farm buildings and facilities, Ken Donald had turned his hand to erecting a new bungalow, though hampered by farm work and slow deliveries.

Haytime this year brought two fresh problems: where to put it, and where to sell it. We had tremendous crops, far, far above anything we have had in the past. From 15 acres we averaged 172 bales per acre, and a weight per acre of 3½ tons at least, sold off the field. 'Given away' might be the more appropriate term, for there is such an abundance that buyers can pick where they please. Only fertilizer was 3 cwt 20-10-10 per acre, or 1 cwt less than normal, but the fields were heavily dressed with broiler muck last autumn.

Our house-building mentioned last month has made little progress. Haymaking has kept us busy, and bricks and windows are in short supply. A five weeks' delivery date for the latter has extended to fourteen weeks now.

The poultry flock is in full production. Laying eggs for broiler hatching, the birds have reached 78 per cent production, and we hope for 80 per cent. One person is fully occupied collecting, feeding, and packing eggs.

First batch of ten lambs was graded two weeks ago, to average 43½ lb carcass weight from 92½ lb liveweight. They were mostly twins from Masham ewes, and did very well. We also killed one for the deep freeze; weighing 84 lb in

Neat green stripes precede a heavy hay crop.

the field, he dressed out at 40 lb, making a really first class carcass expertly cut by our local butcher.

Weaner pigs are now being sold on contract to a feed firm. Bonus for delivery and quantity is helpful, and we are satisfied to date.

In August Ken Donald described the workings of his poultry unit. Large White/Landrace crosses provided the basis of the pig stock, with home-bred gilts retained as replacements. Not until some years later did the farm switch to buying all its hybrid gilts from a large-scale breeding company. An unusual sight in a corn field was recorded. In today's poultry units, the weight of eggs moved weekly is considerable. White Smocks produced eggs for hatching into broiler chicks, and used a specially designed trolley carrying the equivalent of twelve egg cases. Split into compartments each taking six egg trays of thirty eggs, it was wheeled from the egg room to the hydraulic tailboard of the collecting lorry, and raised without effort. Laborious handling of forty-five cases is cut out entirely.

Our 3,100 pullets are laying 77 per cent after peaking at 80 per cent and maintaining that for a fortnight. Last hatchability figures were 85 per cent – very promising at such an early stage. Double-yoked eggs, useless for hatching, can be a problem with this strain, but after reaching 7 per cent the birds are now down to 1 per cent which is much better than reports from some fellow breeders who have suffered 10 per cent. The poultry take virtually one person's time, and my wife and I spend 1½ hours packing eggs each evening.

Weaners from some of our fifty sows have been sold under a new contract scheme, with satisfactory results. Last week we drew a batch of twelve gilts for future breeding; they have two crosses of the Large White boar on Landrace stock.

This system of controlled crossing suits conditions here, and great care is taken in boar selection. At ten weeks these gilts averaged 62 lb, and were taken from litters of 12, 12 and 9.

The Suffolk tup is already running with twenty-five Masham ewes, in the hope for early lambs. Present lambs are doing well, being trough-fed every day, and the first twelve averaged 98 lb liveweight on leaving here. Returns are not yet to hand.

We grow only 12½ acres of corn, now almost ready for harvest. Barley on the potato land went flat after the storms, and a lot of potatoes have grown through. It is an amazing sight; I've never seen anything like it. A fortnight ago, nothing but corn was visible, but the potatoes presumably survived the mild winter, and now thrive where they are not wanted.

A catch crop of fodder radish grazed by Suffolk-cross lambs. The electric fencer (foreground) is much easier to move than nets.

The offending barley field with its hundreds of unwanted potato plants growing through the laid corn proved remarkably easy to deal with, thanks to dry weather. Ken Donald had yet more plans to improve accommodation for sows and litters. Although White Smocks is concerned chiefly with pigs and poultry, field work must also be fitted in by the farmer and his one employee. They had cut the tops off the potatoes three weeks ago, using a pulverizer rear-mounted on the tractor. This also cuts weeds and prevents further disease spores from developing.

We had a busy afternoon among the poultry when they were inoculated against fowl pest for the fourth time. The birds are on deep litter, producing eggs for hatching broiler chicks, and these injections are routine. The hatchery sends two girls, but Len and I pen and catch every hen. It took just four hours. Although we work as quietly as possible, the upset caused a 3 per cent drop in egg output. Still, it's better than getting fowl pest.

Last month I wrote about the state of one barley field, where 'volunteer' potatoes were sprouting through the laid crop. That wonderful weather which was the farmer's salvation made combining far easier and effective than I dared have hoped. The 12½ acres averaged just under 30 cwt per acre, after being hit hard with mildew, and was all under 16 per cent moisture so could be stored in granaries. We also led fifty bales per acre of the driest straw I have ever had.

The lambs have all gone. We have had no returns on the two previous lots, but when the last twenty-four were collected they averaged 95 lb liveweight, apart from two small ones at 66 lb which were quite fleshy. All had been trough-fed for some weeks, which paid hands down.

No great changes to report among the pigs. They come and go, and routine work has sufficed. Plans are afoot to improve some accommodation in what we call the chicken building. It has three pens, with wooden divisions now worn away, and our idea is to split it into six on a more permanent basis.

The new pens will hold a pair of sows and their litters. This has been found the ideal combination after experiments with two, three and four sows and litters. Provided the sows had been mates when running in batches, problems of fighting have not arisen.

A well-earned holiday was taken in July 1973, and then it was a case of straight into haytime. Another example of country people's versatility was highlighted when the poultry transport arrived earlier than scheduled. On an intensive livestock holding something is always happening, keeping the staff on their toes the whole time.

The sheep feeding at a big bale just delivered by tractor.

We had a very full programme before snatching a week's holiday in late June. Our hens had finished their laying period, and a wagon was arranged for 10 p.m. to take 2,550 birds. It arrived at 8 p.m., so I has to chase up my helpers, who fortunately were all at home, and we had all loaded by 10 p.m.

A batch of 550 had gone earlier, to a useful buyer who also takes odd lots, such as those wrongly sexed.

Next morning a man came for the cockerels. This was the day before our departure, and I was out cutting grass at 7.30 a.m., a job I had to leave to load the cocks. The field was then completed, and 8½ acres of grass left to cure in our absence. We started packing at 7 p.m., but our early start next morning did not materialize.

The weather at home was against haymaking, but on the Solway coast we had a marvellous time, with sun and sands for our four young children. By the time we returned, the hay was almost ready to bale.

Len managed wonderfully well in our absence. He had five farrowings, none with less than ten piglets. As he takes a fortnight's holiday in late July/early August, we hope to have the hay tidied and the next batch of chickens settled before then.

A batch of sixty-one weaner pigs was sold in early June, with another thirty or forty due to go. As soon as we see the back of one lot, another batch of sows is farrowing, and we are so short of space that some are multi-suckling, two or three to a building.

Lambs have suffered due to overcrowding. They have had a touch of nemotadirus, but are responding to drenching.

Two fields, each of 7 acres, carry sixty-one ewes and 112 lambs at ten-day intervals, and it is a bit much. Keep is not short; in fact, I bought six little Hereford-cross bullocks and we are still knee-deep in grass.

Frozen pipes play havoc where large numbers of stock are housed, so designs at White Smocks have always had prevention in mind. The new bungalow was ready for occupation in December 1973. A passing mention of a borrowed tup brought a reminder that Ken Donald was happy with his neighbours and his situation; he was not constantly seeking a bigger farm elsewhere.

Our mains water pipes come up through the floor of each building, making them quite safe from frost. The only exception is an outside trough supplying dry sows and young cattle, but cans of hot water soon free it.

Fuel supply is no immediate worry here, as the tanks are full for farm and house. We are delighted with our new bungalow, but are concerned about possible power cuts. If they occur in the New Year they will coincide with peak period of lay for the pullets, which would be disastrous.

December is a busy month among the pigs. We have ten sows to farrow, the first two having fourteen and sixteen; quite a promising start. Our sales are all of strong weaner pigs about ten weeks old, for which a new contract has been worked out. This was an improvement on the old, for meal is £20 a ton up. The cheapest ration costs us £74 a ton, with creep feed for the piglets at over £80.

Our six yearling stirks get a bale of hay a day, sharing an outbuilding with seven dry sows. They all lie together, but go in and out as they please. I had hoped to sell these cattle, but with hay at £30 a ton no one is keen on them. I hope the situation will improve in the spring.

Sheep prices have remained steadier. The ewes should be safely in lamb, with the first lambs due on 11 February. I borrow a tup from a neighbour, who in turn takes mine and his own to run with some gimmer lambs tupped late in the year. Things did not go as I had hoped, and we have prospects of a long, drawn-out lambing-time, when the aim is to complete before potato setting.

This will be our first Christmas in our new home, and the first for four years without having to collect and wash almost 3,000 eggs daily.

A happy potato-picking gang in 1975. Mr Stan Alderson (with cap, behind Ken Donald, centre), was ninety-two years old when this book was published. Andrew and Robin Donald (foreground), aged three and four, carried orange squash up and down the rows on a very hot day.

The charge of 'resting on one's laurels' could never be laid at White Smocks' door. In November 1976 a new farrowing house was described, yet despite care and management a virus infection occurred among the weaner pigs. Then Ken Donald's plan to sell his last lambs to advantage went wrong.

The main job at White Smocks is converting a farrowing house to a new design. Following the experience of three batch farrowings in one new house, I have gone ahead and altered another on practically the same pattern.

It will hold twelve farrowing crates, which give maximum warmth and protection to newly-born piglets. Two local builders are doing the job, and I help when possible.

The biggest job in the conversion is digging the slurry pit. Nothing mechanical can reach the house, so everything has to be done by hand except for a compressor to break the existing concrete on the line of the pit. New floors are being fitted on the existing concrete.

The way feed prices creep up with each order does not lend a lot of confidence to the pig industry, but our recent results have encouraged us to expand. From the last batch of thirteen third-litter sows, we averaged 11.2 born to each litter. As so often happens with livestock, when things go well at one end they do badly elsewhere. We had a certain amount of virus infection among the weaners, cured in three or four days, but not without losing a few piglets.

Egg production among our 3,000 laying birds is nearly 70 per cent but hatchability is 2 per cent less than we would like. The eggs go to breed broiler chicks, and the collection and packing takes one person four hours a day.

Last month I mentioned a forthcoming sale for our remaining lambs, but it never happened. On the morning of the sale there was such a downpour that I could not get onto the field with car and trailer, and also thought there would be few buyers in such atrocious conditions. In the event, however, there had been a very good trade! So the lambs have been wormed, and are going in batches to our local butcher.

Our 6 acre field of winter wheat has been sown at last. The variety is Bouquet, and conditions are not very good, with a wet patch here and there sown by hand.

New Year's Day 1977 saw the first lamb. Its arrival was unscheduled. Ken Donald knew he should have removed the tups in July, but always found something else to do! After the 1976 drought, New Year deluges sought to redress the balance. Mid-winter feed bills reached alarming proportions, but a full-time helper was engaged, giving some respite from the constant routine.

Lambing began on 1 January. This was a mistake: the bulk of our Masham ewes do not start until 1 February, but I left the tups with them during July and took them out too late.

We attach a crayon to the tups' chests so that we can note progress, and when tupping began in earnest, twenty-three ewes remained unmarked. These twenty-three ewes have produced forty-three lambs, all thriving, so it has not turned out too badly after all. Apart from a lamb born dead, there have been no losses so far.

The lambs are now tailed, and are lying out, with the chance to come into part of the yard for shelter. This they use quite a lot.

When I have not been lambing I have been attending to farrowing sows. Over Christmas, twenty-one farrowed in four days, with eight giving birth on Christmas Day. Generally they were very little bother, but the vet was called twice to one with dead piglets inside her. She finished up with four live ones, but it was a reminder of how little in terms of uninterrupted holiday farmers and vets can rely on.

The new farrowing house is almost complete. I am plumbing in the drinking arrangements, which consist of individual nipple drinkers to each sow. It is rather laborious when there is so much routine stock work, but family help enables me to get on.

Egg production from 3,000 broiler breeders is falling off sharply. The birds are due out in six weeks, and I would like the egg production to remain above 50 per cent if possible; it is now 54 per cent.

Then we have just a month for completely cleaning the houses, before starting the cycle all over again with day-old chicks.

The fertilizer is on hand, but I have not ordered seed potatoes yet. Seven acres are usually grown, but I am afraid we shall come a cropper one of these days, with seed prices at more than £400 a ton for good Scotch and 30 cwt needed for each acre. The cost in seed alone is astronomical, and in a favourable growing season there could be a glut. Then the guaranteed price might not reimburse us.

I have never known our fields at White Smocks as wet as they were in February. Ewes with young lambs were absolutely puddled up to their bellies in mud, and one night in desperation I opened the stackyard gate and all available buildings, and let them come inside.

A few hours later, every bit of floor space was taken. Despite this two lambs died, one of them probably succumbing to pneumonia, as its stomach was full.

Of ninety ewes, only a few remain to lamb, the latest tally being not quite 1.75 lambs per ewe. Our son Colin works out lambing percentages to two places of decimals on his calculator.

A load of mangolds has been ordered, and altogether it is a very expensive winter. Our Masham ewes each eat 1½ lb of concentrates a day, plus vast amounts of hay.

With pig meal at £120 a ton, profits are hard to find in that department. The dry sows go on to 8 lb a head after weaning, this alone costing 50p each a day.

The pigs have just been made up to their maximum number with the arrival of the last twelve hybrid gilts. We farrow in batches of twenty-four, and sell the weaners. Although the subsidy of 50p a score does not affect us directly, it is nowhere near what is needed to make pork or bacon pay.

These extra pigs justify a full-time man once more. My wife and family have helped while I have been single-handed, but we had too much work all the time.

Our next big task is cleaning out the deep litter houses, as the breeding hens are only a week away from completing their cycle. One month is allowed for cleaning out and disinfecting, then it's back to day-old chicks again and another batch to rear.

From the last thirteen gilts to farrow, 11.5 piglets to the litter were born alive, of which more than eleven are still alive. Our troubles start at weaning, with a type of coli scour that has resulted in bad losses. Of the last 200 weaners, twenty were lost. Pigs go down with this infection overnight, and

Inside the deep litter house, where these birds produce hatching eggs for broiler chickens.

start to die within twenty-four hours. Though we expect losses where stock are concerned, deaths at such an age are very worrying.

Though breeding programmes were not changed to avoid holidays, in December 1982 the Donald family could look forward to some Christmas respite, with neither matings nor births to attend to. One rogue sow contrived to spoil an otherwise good farrowing.

Fortune is favouring the run-up to Christmas at White Smocks. A batch of over twenty pigs will all have farrowed and been served before the holiday, which should make the work more routine.

That is if all goes well, for farmers and vets know that stock tend to keep their most complicated conditions for just such times.

We are certainly never without a job. The 3,000 laying hens are near the end of their cycle and are down to 50 per cent production but their eggs are still there to collect and pack for the hatchery.

In our spare time we have gutted a range of loose boxes to make an additional seven farrowing pens. Only the plumbing remains to be done, but when these pens are operational the number of sows farrowing in each batch will rise to thirty-one.

Last weekend we took advantage of hard frost to spread slurry from the fattening houses. Then the dry sows were tethered in their stalls ready for artificial insemination. The whole batch was weaned together so came into service more or less on the same day. They have been reduced to nineteen, as the last average was below par. One sow savaged all her piglets except one, bringing the batch average down to 8.5 per litter.

The ewe flock is being housed before Christmas, a job that should be done on a dry day, otherwise the fleeces take a long time to dry. Another essential is that all sheep are eating hay readily outside.

The Masham ewes will be dosed against worms and fluke and walked through the footbath. They should then settle down until lambing.

By June 1984 an adjacent 11 acre field had been purchased, bringing the acreage up to 56. That did not halt continued additions and improvements to the existing homestead. Livestock brought a crop of problems.

Our efforts have been concentrated on finishing the dry sow house. This building has 130 places, which we hope to stock in the New Year. We laid the foundations ourselves, but had the shell erected by contract. Then the stalls

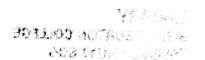

and plumbing were completed by our own labour, helped by a local builder.

We were out for the day on Sunday, and returned to find one pig dead in the fattening house, through fighting. This crops up from time to time and for no apparent reason; some years ago, one particular batch had to be split through incessant fighting, but modern pigs are generally more placid.

Another upset concerned a farrowing gilt who started to savage her piglets as they were being born. We stayed around and gave her an injection to calm her down and she had fifteen in all, eleven of which are still alive. This is an occasional first-litter problem, and the gilt is now behaving normally and probably will in future, but if we hadn't been there we might have lost the lot.

Work among the laying poultry is routine, with egg production declining slowly.

The sheep are eating hay, increased from three to four bales daily during severe frosts.

The ninety-six Masham ewes are due to lamb in early March, and will be housed in January.

Our winter wheat looks well, as do neighbours' crops, and I noticed how very green the December countryside looked one sunny morning.

March 1986 went out like a lion, entailing strenuous efforts to save the newly-dropped lambs. Work had continued throughout the winter on the piggery conversion.

Last Monday was an absolute shocker at White Smocks, where we were faced with a field full of young lambs. Fortunately one of the two deep litter poultry houses was available and we pushed the youngest lambs and their mums inside.

It was also lucky that no lambs were born that day, lambing among our ninety Masham ewes being almost over.

We have had a high proportion of triplets and two sets of quads. This is the first time I have seen four lambs born alive from one ewe and it happened twice. One mother reared all four for a time, until one was sold through the 'Lamb Bank' to another farmer and one was reared on a ewe here. So far, we have had only three single births and nine lambs have been sold as 'pets'.

Sheep are subsidiary to pigs and poultry on this intensive livestock holding and a major task has been to clean out the deep litter house, spreading the manure on the grasses. A skid-steer loader was hired, and a second manure spreader borrowed, enabling us to finish in one day instead of the usual two or three. Then we swept out, and washed all surfaces with a power hose. Near-boiling hot water was used for the final clean; if used earlier, the steam prevents us seeing our mark. Disinfecting and fumigating complete the job.

We have another race against time to complete conversion of the old dry sow house into farrowing quarters. Pens will be ready, but not the plumbing, so water will have to be carried by hand this time.

New Year 1989 brought suitable weather for slurry spreading, and bought-in sheep were doing well. Ken Donald's opinions on Edwina Currie's premature broadside on the egg industry were shared by his fellow poultry producers, who had to pick up the bill for a few careless words. An improvement in pig feeding techniques was recorded.

Ground conditions around the New Year enabled us to continue slurry spreading. Usually the machine can only travel at this season when there is frost. Mild weather has also helped our lambs, still at grass with continuous access to silage.

Last autumn we bought 249 store lambs to feed off surplus grass on this 56 acre intensive livestock holding. To date eighty lambs have been graded, without feeding concentrates. We bought two feeders into which a big bale of silage is dropped every four days. The feeder bars would be ideal for ewes, but are rather too widely spaced for lambs, some of which even creep inside them.

The 3,500 laying birds were sold just before Christmas. The egg rumpus hasn't affected our broiler contracts. A new code of rules for hatcheries was worked out last November, with all food in crumb form – crumbs can only be made through heat treatment. This code was coming out anyway; to trigger off what Edwina Currie triggered off was quite ridiculous.

In the pig section, litters were weaned on three successive days before Christmas. We did as little as possible in Christmas week, but of course had to feed twice a day, and inseminate sows on Boxing Day.

I'm fitting semi-automatic feeders in the sow house. This enables all sows in one row to be fed by pulling a single lever. Then while they are quietly eating, the hoppers are filled for the next feed. Less pandemonium from the pigs and less stress on the operator.

Poultry at White Smocks are taking a lot of time. The new batch of 3,750 birds has been installed, and the egg store extended. We laid a new floor, hygiene being a prime factor, and widened the doors. This was necessary to take the larger egg trolleys which go direct into the incubator. Each trolley holds 4,320 eggs, collected by hand into plastic covered wire mesh buckets, and graded by us before packing onto the trolleys.

These hatching eggs must weigh at least 51 g which, for the first two or three weeks of lay, entails much individual weighing, as the eggs are smaller.

Eggs come in from the automatic nest box system ready for grading. Despite modern facilities
this remains a time-consuming daily job.

The hatchery's transport has a hydraulic tailboard onto which the loaded
trolleys are wheeled for minimum handling.

*In February the Currie shadow loomed over hatching eggs for chicks yet unborn. A
pleasant aspect of real farming was recorded when a life-long hedger made a good job of
a thorn hedge. Ironically, hygiene was a major consideration when the new egg store
became operational in March.*

We are busy on the poultry turn-round. The 3,500 birds have completed their
laying cycle; to be replaced shortly by growing pullets. The object is hatching
eggs for broilers, but we wonder what will happen to the poultry meat market
after Mrs Currie's efforts. Small 56 acre farms like ours can well do without
such knocks.

We took advantage of empty houses to do running repairs. The oldest
building is in its thirtieth season, and is in better order than some newer ones.
I was dubious about these prefabs at the time, but they have amply proved
their worth.

Work is routine among the pigs. We are doing checks on killing-out
percentage by weighing fifteen sample pigs from each load as they leave the

farm. Weighing the entire lorry does not seem accurate enough. A pleasant diversion was receipt of the champion pork carcass cup won at last December's Smithfield Show, now on our sideboard.

Although concentrates are now being fed, almost half our 300 bought-in store lambs graded off grass. We brought 240 indoors just after Christmas, with sixty on pasture that continues to grow.

Some ten or twelve years ago, we planted a thorn hedge beside the orchard. It got away on us, so I asked a local hedge-laying craftsman to layer it for us. Though long retired, he has made a really marvellous job.

A rotary egg cleaner provided another step along the clean egg ladder. The European Poultry Fair convinced Ken Donald and his son Colin of the need for automatic nests, resulting in still cleaner eggs but only after more investment.

Summer holidays are being taken early. My wife and I had a week in Western Scotland, with two glorious days on Skye and a very wet one on Mull. Next week my son and his wife will be away, which means mainly routine work.

On my return the biggest change was in the potatoes, really jumping ahead following welcome rain, and meeting in the rows. Next Friday 21 acres will

The farm garden is Betty Donald's pride and joy.

be cut for hay if the forecast allows, ready for our full staff the following week.

The barley looks very well, and so does the wheat, though it needed spraying against rust. By following the 'tramlines' used during previous spray and fertilizer applications, minimum damage was caused.

Work among poultry is time–consuming, as the birds approach peak lay. Over 2,000 eggs to gather, grade and pack every day. I bought a rotary egg cleaner; a mesh bucket of eggs is inserted in a galvanized bucket of water and anti-bacterial softener. This revolves gently on a circular base, and then back again. Though the majority of eggs come clean from the nests, this gadget is a tremendous help for floor-laid eggs. I wish we had had one years ago.

A bigger investment will be automatic nests as seen at the European Poultry Fair. We plan them for the next crop.

Farrowing among a batch of twenty-two sows is underway.

December of that year brought a welcome stimulus to the endless routine of stock management. Prize cards could be admired during breaks in yet another building programme, this time for bought-in gilts. The stubble turnips mentioned describe themselves; they are sown on a stubble immediately after harvest.

Ken Donald talking to the Queen Mother at Royal Smithfield.

Ken Donald (left) wins the 1988 Royal Smithfield Barclays Bank pork championship presented by Philip Bolam of Barclays.

Royal Smithfield Show provided an exciting climax to our year at White Smocks. Carcass class entries gained fourth in light pork, highly commended in heavy pork, and commended in bacon.

At home, work is continuing on rebuilding accommodation for bought-in gilts. The new layout will be better for the pigs, and easier for use to feed and manage. The gilts stay in this house for four to six weeks between arrival and service, and then a further seven or eight weeks before they go to their farrowing quarters in mid-pregnancy.

We have brought the lambs indoors. They are feeding on silage and hay, but the gates are still left open so they can graze outside. Eight acres of stubble turnips await them. We have not grown this crop before, and growth has been very satisfactory. We have over 300 lambs to feed, using minimum concentrates.

Our winter barley looks well, but winter wheat on the potato land has needed spraying against chickweed.

By 27 April 1991 the new automatic nest boxes had been installed. Only non-stop labour enabled the deadline to be met before the new birds arrived. A son was born and the last of the sheep were sold.

We have been working virtually night and day for weeks. Deep litter poultry house accommodation has been increased from 3,600 to 5,000 birds, automatic nest boxes installed, and the new birds arrive next Monday.

Both houses were extended sideways to give necessary width for the roll-away nest boxes. Eggs roll from the central line of nests on to a conveyor, set in motion once daily to take their cargo into a small egg packing room.

Although contractors installed the nests and extended the buildings, we did most interior work ourselves. The sixteen-year-old feed system needed complete renewal, as did all electric wiring, and bigger extractor fans were installed.

This new system is Dutch and the nearest we could inspect was in Warwickshire. As well as being one of the first, ours is among the smallest, most being installed in very big units.

Amid the upheaval our first grandchild was born, a son for our son Colin, who works the farm with me.

All these happenings have put potato planting back into May. The seed is nicely chitted in trays, and in my experience well-sprouted tubers in a warm seed-bed do extremely well.

The remaining hoggs have not done quite as well as last year, but fifty-two were graded at up to £2.50 per kg. They averaged 19.5 kg and the venture has been worthwhile.

Three generations enjoy a break in 1992.

*The following July the new nests were proving themselves, and another early start was
made to help the wagon driver. A nearby house and 17 acres were bought bringing
White Smocks up to 73 acres but at a price many times that of the original purchase.*

Last Tuesday we had a load of pigs to send, and as the driver was going to the
Great Yorkshire Show he wanted to be at White Smocks at 5.30 a.m. We duly
obliged, quickly loading fifty pigs aged five months and averaging 70–5 kg
liveweight. Our pens were rather full, and so we drew out three or four from
each.

Our son determines the size of pig we need, weighs it and marks it and then
marks a few identical ones. By dint of constant practice he is rarely wrong, and
this method results in far less stress on pigs and men than weighing the lot.

After experimenting with a single space feeder, we have installed one in
each of twenty-four fattening pens. The pig's nose goes into the feed, and it is
completely enclosed like a horse in blinkers, so is not challenged by other
pigs. Food is ad lib and always fresh, and the shy pigs and the smaller ones do
better.

Having recently bought a nearby house with 17 acres of land our total
acreage has risen to 73. This involved extra haytime, but all 32 acres were
secured in June, and nearly 4,500 bales made without a spot of rain.

Big round silage bales being made by a contractor.

Poultry are almost at peak lay, with the new automatic nest boxes working well. Floor eggs are only 3 per cent of total, due to prompt removal in the early stages.

Another year passed and son Colin, who wrote this diary, was playing an even bigger part in running the farm, while Ken Donald concentrated on renovating the recently acquired farmhouse.

The new lot of laying birds is near peak production. Though they are laying at 77 per cent, we would like them to top 80 per cent. The automatic nest boxes work better with each crop, as we learn the wrinkles.

Very hot weather is not good for intensive stock for, although they live in a controlled environment, we can only draw in warm air for them.

Potatoes are nicely through. Our aim was to spray them just as they appeared, but weather conditions prevented that and the later spray caused slight scorching.

In one wet place on some new ground, the Estima have not appeared. That variety has a tendency to rot off in wet conditions and I haven't yet dug down to see what is happening. With my mother and father in Wales, our apprentice

Ken Donald and his son Colin (right) with the Smithfield Pork Carcass Cup.

and I have our hands full with routine feeding and egg collection on this 73 acre livestock holding. We did manage to go round the hedgebacks with the knapsack sprayer to spray thistles and nettles, a job that is apt to be missed.

A batch of nineteen sows was weaned last week. They averaged nine piglets reared per litter, and have been served this week. In hot weather we try to reduce stocking densities.

At the initial European Pig and Poultry Fair in Warwickshire we noticed a big swing away from intensive conditions. Even where pigs are kept inside, designs are changing, and there is a lot to keep up with.

CURRER HEIGHTS

The milk producer/retailer forms a strong segment of Yorkshire farming, to be found in few other counties. The milk roundsman bottling milk from his own cows grew up with the industrial West Riding, and many a farming family turned their few upland acres to maximum potential by selling their product from door to door. The milk round was the forerunner of the 'added values' strategy now advocated by leading economists.

Because of this extra value of home-produced milk, West Riding cows graze pastures that in other counties would be deemed suitable only for store cattle and sheep. Jim Scott's Currer Heights farm is lower down than some, but is not easy land to farm. Its 130 acres are no longer generally regarded as

Jim and Nora Scott with Bibby representative John Binns (right) taking part in a publicity campaign in the late 1970s.

Timber trusses that have stood the test of time in the buildings.

an economic unit, yet when 'The Year Round' started the acreage was under two-thirds the present size.

When economists quote minimum acreage figures, they reckon without the man. Jim Scott is a forthright West Ridinger, given to strong views, deriding politicians who, he claims with ample justification, do not do their job as well as he does his. When the BSE cattle scare was threatening red meat sales, he was so incensed by misleading propaganda that he sought to prove the safety of beef by eating no other meat for weeks on end!

Currer Heights is sited no great distance from Leeds/Bradford airport and the busy trunk roads that service it. Pass through the farmhouse and into the pleasant series of gardens, and another world opens up. A sweep of green valley fringed with ever-encroaching houses provides grazing for a herd of dairy cattle whose milk is bottled on the premises. As early as June 1965, changing habits in the urban population necessitated rescheduling work in the dairy. Trouble from dogs, sadly part of life on 'the urban fringe', was recorded.

The homestead at Currer Heights is set snugly into the hillside; it is seldom possible to build on the level in Airedale. The fields in the foot of the valley may be subject to flooding from the Aire, though less so than in years gone by. There are obvious advantages in siting farm buildings in the centre of the holding, but in pre-tractor days that was not the only consideration. The

A winter scene over fields at Currer Heights, viewed from the farm garden.

The scene in summer. Drystone walls
take hours of upkeep yearly, but form
valuable shelter.

farmstead's position should make life for horses as easy as possible. Carting work was two-way: farmyard manure out, hay, corn, straw and roots in. To build on top of a hill helped manure leading, but meant an uphill struggle when bringing home the crops. The reverse applied to the valley bottom, for even on a grassland holding where neither roots nor corn were grown there was considerable carting.

Currer Heights is approached from Gill Lane. It has a sign at the end of a farm lane flanked by drystone walls and fringed with daffodils which Jim Scott and his wife, Nora, augment each autumn. These 80 yd of farm road open onto a sloping yard, with Ghyll Fold House immediately ahead. This imposing dwelling has no connection with the farm, and bears the date 1649. Jim Scott believes that his house is at least as old, with its smaller mullioned windows and immensely thick internal stone walls.

Its rear entrance is unprepossessing, with a steep flight of steps leading to a long, low building, part cellar and lit mainly by electric light. This invaluable room contains a neat conglomeration of outdoor clothing, boots, garden equipment and general domestic stores.

The dwelling proper begins only on leaving this junction between house and farm. A large living kitchen has its ovens and sink units, and a table to accommodate the many callers, be they family, friends, or business visitors connected with the farm. The comfortable sitting-room with its prints and family photographs leads to the dining-room, whose centrepiece is a large dark oak dining table, designed to seat eight but which frequently seats up to fourteen. Nora Scott delights in entertaining family and friends, and the room's atmosphere has gained from these many convivial gatherings.

Recently an adjoining farm of 48 acres has been taken over, making life very full and interesting. It is all grass, and lower down the valley than this, so we hope for better crops.

Government policy statements give little confidence when one gets down to the job of applying them to the individual farm. Which is most needed, milk, beef, or corn? I do not know, but am now rearing all calves to use some of the extra acres.

. Recent figures indicate that Ayrshire bull calves may be reared economically, and cows not used to breed replacements are crossed with Angus or Charolais.

Customers are all back from holiday, so the retail round has settled down again. Increased egg prices in shops have led to bigger demand for ours, for we go the year round on only two price levels and have not yet applied the winter one.

Grasses are usually top-dressed with nitrogen during the last week in August, at forty units per acre, but this year sixty units were applied experimentally on 9 September. November grass is a very valuable commodity.

The electric fence is still being moved twice daily and the only concentrates fed are at 2 lb per gallon above the second gallon, plus one pound 'tying up' feed that all receive.

A pneumonia case is recovering, but slowly. She eats only a limited amount of cake, and soon refuses any increase. Newly calven cows keep on milking, and lose condition so quickly when not eating properly. This wet summer may make dairy cows more ailment-prone, their bodies and the grass suffering from lack of sunshine.

Chief between-milkings job is cleaning out the calf pens. We seem to have calves all over the place except where they should be. Then we shall start muck-leading from the fold yard, as only in autumn are we able to lead onto the land direct.

In August 1965 Jim Scott spoke of the stable milk price compared with rising servicing costs, and took a typical swipe at the Milk Marketing Board (MMB).

Silage making is now completed at Currer Heights, and the 300 ton clamp rolled down and sealed. Under our wide-span barn we find that plastic sheet covered with straw bales gives the best seal, especially if some rough grass is used to top out with. The same sheet has been used for four years, and if any rips occur it seems quite effective to lie a plastic fertilizer bag over the tear.

Lime makes a cheap and easy seal, but trouble arises in removing it in winter, especially if snow and wet prevent access to the land. Spasmodic spreading means that parts of the field get too much, while others are missed, and the clamp always seemed to need more top taking off on Saturday mornings!

Trouble from dogs is an ever-present worry on this dairy farm. The other night a dozen strong heifer calves were turned out to grass for the first time, and next morning they were found on the other side of a strong barbed wire fence.

One calf had very badly cut shoulders. They had evidently been terrified, and had charged the wire in a neck of the field. Luckily, no more damage was done. Please do keep your dogs under control!

Strain 19 vaccine against contagious abortion is used on all heifer calves between four and eight months. This scheme is free, and it is disappointing that the response is so poor. The first year I came here four abortions occurred. We have had none for three years now, which seems positive indication of its value.

As soon as possible after the silage cut each field received a further dressing of nitro-chalk, 2 cwt per acre for grazing, and 3 cwt where another cut is to be taken. Drought soon hits this south-facing farm, and recent rains were welcome.

My cowman takes his holidays next week. Cow identification is a big problem for the relief milker, as several animals look very much alike in a herd of fifty home-bred Ayrshires. The herdsman knows them by a spot of colour or setting of udder, but detailed written instructions must be left for others.

Large eartags of aluminium alloy are being tried, and can be read from some yards distance. Something better still may come from the Milk Marketing Board's £500 for the best idea.

Changing holiday habits bring more problems to the producer-retailer. Twenty years ago, a week's holiday was a big event, and the milkman knew about it some time beforehand. Now he usually finds a little note saying that the family is away for two or three weeks, and consequently has drastically to rearrange his bottling requirements.

Although retail milk has gone up ½d a pint recently, there has been very little grumbling from customers. Over the past three years, price to consumers has gone up by only 5 per cent, yet at Currer Heights our electricity costs 100 per cent more, and water 300 per cent more, over the same period.

This water question is becoming really serious. Here we are in one of the wetter districts of the country, yet we pay 3s 9d per 1,000 gallons. Small West Riding producer–retailers like ourselves use a vast quantity in the vital tasks of cooling milk and cleaning buildings and equipment. Were it not for the good fortune of having a private supply for cattle at grass, water bills would be astronomical.

One newly-calved cow has gone down with pneumonia, an all too common occurrence at this season. We tend to think 'It's summer – she'll be alright', whereas the shock of calving may precipitate the illness at any time.

We are rather puzzled by an outbreak of coughing among the cows, showing especially if they are hurried. It is not husk, and veterinary tests of saliva and dung have proved negative, nor do we have any racing stable connections! No doubt a sunny spell would bring a cure.

Servings of maiden heifers continue, but there have been rather more repeats with cows than usual. I am trying to reduce the calving index, but this is one of the most difficult of the cowman's jobs. Hence MMB's latest Low Cost Production report seems a little futile.

They stress that on most farms calving intervals are too long, and milking machines less than 100 per cent efficient. Every dairy farmer in the country knows this, but what is to be done?

Variable quality rubber used in teat liners is beyond our control, and the whole milking system cannot be checked every day. It is a very big job to find just where vacuum is being lost, and when ours was tested in summer it was reasonably satisfactory.

Pullets which started laying last summer have now reached 80 per cent, and prospect of temporarily better prices is some recompense for those who stuck to hens during the lean years.

Customers return from holiday next week, and when our rounds girl finishes hers, staff routine will settle down to normal.

In lighter vein, the family 'donned up to the eyes' to attend a wedding last week. This is something most people enjoy but farmers probably more than others, and this occasion of much fun and merriment was all the more appreciated as we were not concerned with the arrangements.

The farmhouse at Currer Heights was the focal point of the retail round, with frequent phone calls concerning deliveries. The whole farm played its part in educating urban visitors in the ways of the countryside, as described in this diary in late May 1971.

Yellow stubble contrasting with heavy, green sward denotes the forage harvester's passage on Yorkshire's grassland areas at this season. Timing of the

A place for everything. . . . Ropes and chains must be kept handy for emergencies.

operation has a marked effect on next winter's milk yields, and at Currer Heights the crops are rather better than last year.

A retail round complicates farm organization, as all jobs which might crop up during a busy spell like silage making must be cleared first. We therefore start silage when the farm allows us, rather than when we might wish.

Grasses freed from stock all winter are good, but those which were spring grazed are a little light. We went round the lot with twenty units of nitrogen, using more on the mowing fields. One 6 acre was grazed bare and then received all the muck from the loose housing, plus forty units of nitrogen per acre. It should make a useful cut for hay or silage.

The silage pit is cleaned out, as are both poultry and calf houses. I have invested in a new grass mower, a two-drum type, choosing a foreign one against my usual principles. The reason is that it is the best I can buy locally, and for such a vital machine, on-the-spot servicing is essential.

Almost all stock is outside now, looking very well these nice sunny evenings. Low protein grazing nuts are actually costing me more than did the complete dairy ration throughout winter, for which my merchant stuck to his contract price fixed last September.

Dales farmyards are soon filled by modern machinery. Here the milk bulk tanker is about to leave, with forage wagon and tractor in the background.

Our last meeting of the old Agricultural Executive Committee took place recently. Representation is said to be continuing, but I can't see liaison with the Minister being anything like as close as in the past.

A local Young Farmers' Club (YFC) looked over the farm one evening, as did a class of seven-year-olds one morning. Several sent letters of thanks. One read:

> See the cows all eating hay,
> For the hay he need not pay.
> He grows it all, all by himself,
> Until in winter it's on the shelf.

This youngster's views on the economics of grass preservation may not be strictly accurate, but contain a basis of truth which we shall all be working to fulfil during the coming weeks.

Jim Scott puts first things first, whether he is questioning the speaker at a National Farmers' Union meeting, addressing the many urban gatherings where he puts over the countryman's point of view, or deciding farm policy. First of all he is a cowman. He likes top-class cattle and good food for them. Whether the latter is secured by a fleet of the latest silage machines or by an antiquated forage wagon is of no importance to him. He believes that returns from dairying do not warrant 'keeping up with the Joneses' by investing heavily in new tackle. He recorded another successful campaign in 1971.

Hay and silage crops of good quality but less than average weight are commonplace in Yorkshire this year. Those at Currer Heights, on the fringe of the West Riding industrial belt, are no exception to the rule.

We finished silage in good time, but with about three-quarters of the amount required to see us through next winter. Haytime was also begun, and then delayed to get more weight.

This policy didn't work, however, as what rain there was proved sufficient to stop haymaking, but not enough to make grass grow.

Our plan is to cut 30 acres for second-crop silage. Here again we may become unstuck, for if there is no appreciable downpour we may have to turn the cows in. At the moment we are living from hand to mouth, moving stock around to clear up as best we can.

Despite these tribulations, the cattle look very well. These constant moves all take up time, however, and we are having to feed heavily to maintain yields. From May to September in a normal year we only feed 1 lb per cow.

At present the ration is 3 lb per gallon, or more than in winter with access to the silage face. It is very expensive, but there is no alternative. If yields drop now, they never recover.

One lot of hens has gone out, and been replaced by pullets. In any spare time, we have been setting new gate posts, fencing, and mowing rubbish. Deep-rooted docks and thistles grow whatever the weather.

I am thinking about cubicles for the cows next winter. This is simply because sawdust supplies are restricted. Second-hand timber and no grant may work out cheaper than new stuff, grant-aided. Another new building will be necessary in any case.

Farmers' meetings have almost stopped for the summer. Occasionally I walk round with the gun after tea, as a few rabbits have reappeared. Some have been shot, and the dog got one last night.

Only one thing disappointed me about the Great Yorkshire Show: the King's Troop Royal Horse Artillery has not been on display for a few years now. I would go twice if they returned.

The forage wagon that picked up mown grass from the swathe in one operation sufficed, and fitted in with the system. Jim Scott and his one man, Andrew, had up to seventy cows to milk, and calves to feed. That happened every morning and evening regardless of other work, and there was never any question of neglecting routine in order to get more hours in the silage field. A spell in the middle of the day, and again in the evening, resulted in a steady accumulation of grass in the silo. The resulting lack of summer leisure was recorded in July 1969.

One man was on holiday during Great Yorkshire Show time, so I did not manage to get there. Silage making has finished with rather a struggle. After the first fine week, we seemed to be knocked off every other day for weather, as I do not like to lead wet grass into the clamp.

We got bogged down with one load when it was crossing the track of a water main laid last winter. As often happens, trench filling had been carelessly done, and we had to suffer for it.

We have also tried to make a little hay, not too successfully. I have said before that I don't know why we bother. Two loads of straw have arrived to cover the silage top, costing £2 a ton more than last year.

The only chance I have had to ride my horse was when taking her from one field to another! Otherwise we have been going flat out with our main harvest of the grassland year – silage – and are already contemplating the second cut in August.

A fresh batch of 500 point-of-lay pullets arrived, and laid a few eggs

The lowing herd winds slowly up to the milking parlour.

immediately. They are now above sixty a day. Egg trade on the retail round remains remarkably good, better than the milk.

This is a difficult time of year on the round; people no longer take the one definite week's holiday, but are liable to up and off at any time for any period. Most let us know in good time, but occasionally we have to trail up the garden path for nothing, or find some dozey tale we can't make anything of. 'Away, Don't know how long. If not back Tuesday leave milk Wednesday' !!

The Minister of Agriculture is equally confusing with this business of putting certain grades down a halfpenny for so long, then up a penny. Typical Government flattery of the public, using an industry to try and make the public appreciate what their rulers do.

In June 1970 he was still busy with silage making, still trying to keep elderly machines at work, and waxing sarcastic about the Milk Marketing Board.

Though we are well on with silage making, having some 40 acres in the clamp, crops are disappointingly light. Meadows are normally grazed to 12 May, then fertilized and closed. The result every year till now has been a dense crop of new growth. This time we have had to cut into fields reserved for hay in order to fill the silo.

I am sure that some fertilizer has been wasted; crops cannot grow without water. It is interesting to note that the meadows receiving farmyard manure have withstood the drought best; perhaps those of us who have stuck to the muck cart are not so daft after all.

The cows are not milking too badly, despite heavy stocking. Trouble is that there has been no regrowth behind either them or the forage harvester.

We have had the usual troubles during silage making; part of the trailer frame welding snapped, so I had to work until dark last Sunday to mend it ready for a prompt start.

More serious was the forage harvester axle, due simply to metal fatigue and our inability to replace the machine as planned because of expenditure on a muck spreader through accident.

Folk on the retail round are starting to go on holiday; we learn to cope with this one year by year. Poultry are dropping off a bit, with 500 new pullets due shortly.

Buttercups and docks were sprayed satisfactorily. Rabbits are increasing surprisingly, so I shall have to be after them.

My one outing in the month was to Arundel Castle, where we had a warm welcome and tour of the estate, well explained by the Duke of Norfolk's manager. I'll bet they have suffered with the drought.

An MMB Press report stresses advisability of keeping a month's fodder reserve. Generations of farmers have known this, but to apply it with modern stocking and interest rates is almost impossible. MMB has a genius for bringing out and dusting things that others were taught fifty years ago!

Livestock people all know the worry of fodder stocks disappearing at an alarming rate, and wondering if they will last till the spring grass grows. In February 1986 a spell of strong sunshine revived spirits, though uncertainty over the new milk quotas clouded the business outlook.

The best news from Currer Heights is that silage and hay stocks should now last until spring. Like other dairy farmers, we began the winter in a rather precarious position, unsure that all hungry mouths would be filled before the grass grew again.

Some third-rate hay turned out better than I expected; the cattle eat it well and there is no dust. It must have been very dry after initial weathering.

The second-cut silage clamp contains a foot-thick layer of soily material.

Currer Heights dairy herd at the silage face. A barrier in front of the face helps control feeding, and straw is stacked on top.

Silage above and below it is first class and this bad patch must have been caused when trailers got stuck in last summer's misery, and we had to haul them free. Grass picked up in such circumstances is inevitably contaminated.

Last weekend we had two glorious days on these West Riding fields. Instead of hanging around the silage face and sheds, all cows were basking and blinking their eyes in the sun-drenched yard.

I watched them for some time in my shirt sleeves, seeking any in bulling. We have had difficulty lately in catching cows for service; those we don't want to breed from again seem always in bulling, while the others we want to show no signs. A change of minerals is indicated.

Treacle is being fed from rollers which the cows lick. It was introduced years ago to combat slow fever or acetonaemia, and works. That's more than I can say of quotas, which remain confusing. Retail and wholesale milk sales are lumped together for quota, but the figures never come together, so I don't know exactly how we stand.

In October 1987 came more indication of the widespread readership and family feeling engendered by 'The Year Round'. In the same month was a reminder that livestock husbandry still has its physical hazards, and requires stockmanship of a high order.

Last month's mention of difficulties in obtaining corrugated curved sheeting to repair our Currer Heights barn brought a welcome response. After an offer from a fellow farmer, I journeyed complete with trailer to his farm near the Lancashire border.

After losing my way, I arrived to a warm welcome from the farmer and his wife, and an excellent lunch. Their farm at 1,000 ft made me appreciate our own lower West Riding grassland holding.

The barn roof has been duly repaired and looks much improved. Though normally not particularly noticeable, the hole in the roof caught the eye from all the surrounding countryside.

Another episode that ended happily concerned six yearling heifers. They had broken onto the road when seeking shelter from a heavy shower, and a passer-by had evidently put them into a nearby field. This happened to contain our Angus bull and his bunch of bulling heifers. Strange though it may seem, when we walked through the gate to retrieve a fairly desperate situation, the six strays separated themselves from the rest and dashed towards us. No doubt our bull felt on top of the world when his extra harem arrived, but he gave them up without turning nasty, as some bulls would.

Cubicle house doors are now left open for the cows at night, and the cubicles are usually fully occupied in the mornings. A little hay is fed in them to entice the heifers and familiarize them with dairy routine.

Sudden deaths can still occur among cattle, but veterinary science has reduced them, as outlined in May 1988. Field names have grown up over the years for all sorts of odd reasons; here's a pleasant example.

Grass is growing quite well at Currer Heights, which rather surprises me as I expected soil reserves to be depleted after last summer's tremendous growth. Our biggest problem is the amount of 'poaching' where cattle were outwintered.

We fertilized and chain-harrowed the 20 acre where the black Angus bull and his heifers wintered. It was certainly a bit of a mess and we must drive carefully when we cut for hay. Another difficult area was trenched 8 ft deep for sewage pipes and, although the soil was reinstated, the drains don't work as well as before.

After grazing that field a few years ago, we lost two cattle from blackleg. There seems no successful treatment for this soil-borne disease and we now vaccinate against it. The deaths occurred after the beasts were moved elsewhere, so were inconclusive, but I suspected that deep stirring of the soil had something to do with it.

Some of our fields are named after their acreage, but an 11 acre one opposite the house is known as Yonder Field. When our eldest son was very small he would ask for our two men, Mr Dennis and Mr Myers, who happened to be working 'across yonder' at the far side of the field. To this day it is called Yonder Field from a name that cropped up thirty-two years ago.

Checking machinery after use is standard practice on well-run farms, but not all admit when they have slipped up. Jim Scott did just that in May 1990, and continued his precautions against a killer cattle disease. Farmers were becoming really dispirited by constant public and media attacks on their work; Jim Scott had the knowledge and opportunity to put the record straight.

Make hay while the sun shines, says an old saying usually used out of context. We should be doing just that in silage and hay fields at Currer Heights, but holidays delayed the start. Bulk should be adequate even if quality is not of the highest.

During a trip up the Dales I saw a few fields cut, but crops not heavy as yet. We have brought out our silage machinery, only to find once again that

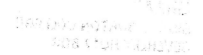

Jim Scott in typical pose watching the hay baler and bale sledge at work.

however carefully it is checked when put away something always seems to be wrong in spring. A new buckrake tine is needed, and some other spares which I thought were on hand.

Cattle have been injected against blackleg, a soil-borne disease that struck without warning a few years ago. The young cattle have all been ear-tagged with individual and herd numbers under the Ministry's tuberculosis and brucellosis eradication schemes.

No one gives us credit for having conquered these diseases; all we hear are anti-farming publicity seekers who lace their statements with falsehoods and untruths. In the last war notices stated 'Careless talk costs lives'. Today careless talk causes illness and anxiety among the farming community.

A tree surgeon has been dealing with branches overhanging a neighbour's garden. One big branch snapped off in the gales and lodged where it might have dropped on our cattle, so we have sawn it up and taken it home.

In February 1992 the economic difficulties of farming in the Dales were underlined. Jim Scott mastered a difficult calving single-handed, then again poked fun at the superior attitude of city mentalities.

We are proceeding very nicely towards spring at Currer Heights, with the birds singing and daffodils popping through. Mid-January to late February can bring the year's most dangerous weather in my experience.

Silage and hay should last until the grass grows. The further the cows eat into the clamp, the better the silage. That is as expected; the last to be eaten was the first to go in last June.

It is always difficult to catch cows a-bulling in winter. I spotted two after 10.30 one morning, the latest time for Milk Marketing Board to accept calls. However, I was given the number of another farmer on the inseminator's route, who said he would pass on my message. No one came, and I was just a little perturbed at losing two services.

In between milkings we have been replacing the heel board in one set of cow cubicles, quite a major job. One cow began to calve at 9.00 p.m. and by 11.00 p.m. had made no progress. I had to calve her myself by dint of cords to the feet slung round my back. Those cords that tie bags of bailer twine together make ideal calving ropes.

On TV recently they showed a very old cow at calving. When she actually calved, she had miraculously changed into a much younger one. TV people think that because they can't tell one cow from another, no one else can!

A month later he underlined the extra economic difficulties of farming in the dales.
Emmerdale Farm is filmed close to Currer Heights, but Jim Scott was not impressed
by the technicians' knowledge of those country crafts so often taken for granted. He
recorded both sides of farming near a town.

Grass here has been green all winter, but is not yet growing. Daffodils and polyanthus are colouring the garden, and grassland has received the first nitrogen dressings, but the cows remain on full winter rations.

Fortunately there is ample silage to last until grass time. I hoped we had sufficient straw, but had to buy another load. A wagon can carry only 5 tons where it could take 15 or 20 tons of corn or fertilizer, making straw a dear commodity along the Pennine lanes.

A TV crew has been filming one of our gates and field. They needed a gate with a sneck, whereas this one had a chain, so they asked to fit a new fastener. Of course I said yes. However, they started by fixing the keeper to the gate and the sprung handle to the post – the wrong way round. To set two stout posts and a gate that swings shut is a countryman's art, and not one they had mastered.

Regular readers may recall when we had so many bull calves that heifer replacements became scarce. Now we have had eight heifers in a row; never in my life have I seen so many.

Thieves attempted to steal stone slates from an off-building, but were caught and the slates replaced. On a happier note, two classes of children from the local school came to look at the stock. A newly-born calf caused quite a stir.

Then in May 1993 came the final decision. Jim and Nora took the plunge and organized a sale of live and dead stock which would enable them to retire from full-time farming. There was not only the wrench of parting from the cattle they had bred and nurtured for so long, but the cessation of monthly diaries as part of 'The Year Round' team for twenty-eight years without a break.

I always said I would retire from farming Currer Heights when I couldn't do two men's work in a day. That situation arose years ago, but milking cows and bottling milk in the tradition of West Riding producer-retailers is quite a big job. With apologies to Lewis Carroll: 'The time has come to sell the lot, 'Cos youth no longer lingers in the wings.'

We reached our decision quite quickly, and the sale of live and dead stock takes place here next Tuesday.

Friends tell me that dairy cattle from this 130 acre West Riding grassland holding are bound to sell well. Machinery is being prepared and, though we have never gone in for a lot of expensive tackle, all is in working order. Someone might even buy the milking parlour fittings installed thirty-one years ago!

The cows are milking very well, and grass growth has been quite splendid. Earlier we had a bitterly cold spell.

'When the wind is in the east, 'Tis good neither man nor beast.' Our cows agreed, standing huddled up under the stone walls.

It was very noticeable how warm the sun was when standing in a sheltered corner of the farmyard, while at the gate opening into the paddocks it was absolutely perishing. That's a tribute to the design of these old farmsteads.

Most of the young stock are out now, a great relief after a long winter of foddering.

After sixty busy years in dairy farming, I shall sample the interests and pleasures of retirement following the sale of implements and livestock at Currer Heights.

Fortunately the sale day was fine and dry, among some much worse weather.

We milked the cows as usual, and came to breakfast with appetites diminished.

Sale day scene, with winter quarters for cattle on the right.

Then the bustle of the day started, with streams of interested and interesting people. Some I knew, others introduced themselves as readers who have followed the doings of Currer Heights for twenty-eight years.

Implements and fixed equipment sold reasonably; cattle were pleasing to the eye, behaved well and sold well.

Loading continued far into the evening, with amusing incidents. A Land Rover and trailer were parked down the slope, and when the cattle stood on the ramp, this tipped up the trailer front and the back of the Land Rover. Fortunately the cattle retreated and the whole outfit came to earth with a bang.

On the whole the sale went champion. I take the opportunity to thank my wife, family, auctioneers and helpers who guided me through one of the saddest days of my life.

Though not a drinking man, I raise a glass of best Scotch to all who attended, and to the many friends made through 'The Year Round'.

Jim Scott supervising the arrival of a load of hay at Currer Heights.

BRINK TOP

When Jim Scott retired from farming at Currer Heights, another West Riding dairy farmer was needed. He or she should preferably be a producer-retailer, given to outspoken opinions. Michael Mallinson volunteered, and seemed to have all the attributes necessary for the successful continuation of the column. In September 1993 he described his high-lying holding only a few miles from Halifax.

Brink Top, a West Riding dairy farm high on the Pennines, is the latest holding to be included in this column. A farmer visitor once said: 'There's nothing between here and the Rockies'. Certainly, the prevailing south-westerly winds can be very strong.

This farm's happenings are recorded in 'The Year Round' in succession to Currer Heights, whose farmer retired recently.

Brink Top's 280 acres are owner-occupied, while another 100 rented acres include some Water Board land. The 1,000 ft contour runs through the yard where 100 cows are milked. Then the land runs all the way to a level shelf at between 800 and 900 ft, to rise again above 1,200 ft.

Milking is not our biggest job. It is the bottling and retailing that takes the time. In the present economic climate all this extra effort seems worthwhile, especially with the demise of the Milk Marketing Board.

There are five of us – myself, my son, a tractor driver here for many years, an equally conscientious herdsman and a trainee. My son and I each live in seventeenth-century weavers' houses. Our 245 cattle include a suckler herd of thirty, all home-bred crosses from the dairy herd. We also have a small sheep flock of fifty including lambs. Present job between milkings is re-seeding a field where foundry waste sand was dumped years ago.

Tragically, this ideal solution was not to be. Michael Mallinson died suddenly, even before his second contribution could be written. Despite the shock and upheaval, his son Guy stepped into the breach and is keeping the flag flying.

One of the younger generation, Guy is a dedicated breeder of high-yielding dairy cows and also determined to make his suckler herd pay. With an eye for a bargain in second-hand equipment, he likes to keep his farm up to date mechanically.

Stormy weather has at last driven the cows inside at Brink Top. During early November's still, mild days, they lay out quite happily, despite having access to self-feed silage and opportunity to use the cubicle house. This is bedded with shavings, in ready supply only 3 miles away.

The gateways are now a sea of mud, and grass on this West Riding dairy farm has stopped growing, but we made 600 big silage bales. There should be ample winter fodder, though we have had no straw delivered yet.

Demand for milk on the retail round is holding up. We producer-retailers fight a hard battle, especially if supermarkets use milk as a loss leader.

The calf trade is good. Prices for finished stock are down, and store cattle are a bit disappointing, but newly calven cows have gone through the roof. At one time we could replace a geld cow by adding £200 to her price, but it now takes three fat cows to buy one replacement.

We always seem to have two-thirds bulls born. It's unbelievable. We nominate sires through AI, selecting them very very carefully to suit our conditions. The aim is a big, strong-boned animal with an udder well up out of the mud, but these plans go awry if few heifers are born.

Temperament is also important. With one man milking a batch of six or seven, he simply cannot do with a heifer that repeatedly kicks off the machine.

We are in the fortunate position at Brink Top of having more than one set of buildings. At weaning the cows are kept out of earshot of their calves, making life quieter.

There is both a dairy herd and a suckler herd on this West Riding upland farm. The first home-bred Simmental-cross heifers for the suckler herd are due to calve in February and March. Their sire is a pale-coloured bull whose calves have a very saleable Continental look.

I bought a large trough on wheels which feeds thirty-two cows. It is filled with silage cut from the top of the clamp above cow height, using a block cutter bought at a farm sale.

A batch of dairy heifers has been injected to bring them into season all together.

Guy Mallinson and his wife, Caroline, with their family.

Contributors and their wives after twenty-eight years of 'The Year Round'. The scene is at Friars' Hagg in August 1993.

Over the past five years we have consistently had more bulls than heifers born. Someone somewhere is getting my share of heifers! A good newly-calven heifer now costs £1,000, a lot of money to find.

All forty-two sheep have been tupped.

We're having a blitz on the old stone land drains, using the farm tractor-mounted digger and a shovel. A number of blocked places have been freed.

There was an electrical fault during milking. After switching on various items, the fault was traced forty minutes later to the immersion heater.

CHESTNUT FARM

Standing snugly on the flat and fertile Vale of York, Chestnut Farm is a typical village holding. It abuts the historic church at Sutton on the Forest, York, and, inevitably with village farms, has several fields at a distance from the homestead. Its true name is Laurence House Farm, not Church Farm as might be expected; Laurence Sterne, author of *Tristram Shandy*, was reputed to have lived here after his vicarage was burnt down.

Philip Ward, his wife, Peggy, and daughters, Judith and Charlotte, enjoyed village life at Chestnut Farm. Philip was one of the original diarists: meticulous, enthusiastic, a forward-looking practical farmer and a keen churchman. Sadly, he died of cancer at a comparatively young age. His invaluable contributions spanned ten years.

Chestnut Farm was 200 acres. Its typical mixed cropping included potatoes, sugar beet and cereals. A poultry unit supplied eggs for sale at the door, and beef cattle were yarded each winter.

Philip Ward always had his diary prepared on time, and it was difficult to imagine him being late for anything. He worked closely with the National Agricultural Advisory Service (NAAS), forerunner of the present Agricultural Development and Advisory Service (ADAS).

A very early diary in July 1965 told of Philip Ward seeking Ministry advice on a mineral deficiency to which the farm's lighter soils were subject. The area was once part of the ancient Forest of Galtres, and from the top of Sutton Bank much of the Vale appears covered with trees. A true countryman, Philip Ward appreciated one reason why farmers removed hedges.

Haymaking does not occupy the same important place on this Vale of York arable holding as it does on a hill sheep farm.

We are principally concerned at Chestnut Farm with gathering a sufficiency of bulky fodder to provide maintenance for fattening bullocks during winter, and do not attempt early-cut high protein samples so beneficial to the dairy farmer. Nor does our system warrant anything beyond run-of-the-mill tackle for 26 acres. Mower, tedder, baler, a bit of wind and sun and this mature herbage is soon dry.

If possible, cutting starts on Thursday or Friday, with the idea of making the crop safe during the following week, with no weekend work, and so it worked out this year.

An interesting case arose on one of the light land barley fields. The crop was obviously not thriving, and manganese deficiency was suspected. However, the NAAS Regional Soil Chemist diagnosed lime deficiency, although a test last March was apparently satisfactory.

The crop was already a foot high, and I feared that the lime wagons would do much damage, but it was that – or a crop failure. One ton of ground lime-stone was applied per acre, and by now the wheelings have disappeared, and the crop completely recovered.

sugar beet has now been hoed the second time over, but had to be sprayed against aphis. When we scruffled for the last time, we used an attachment which sows 1 cwt nitro chalk along the rows. Factory fieldsmen may disagree, but I like plenty of top on beet; it attracts moisture and shades the roots.

The Record and Majestic potatoes look well, and are rowed up and finished with. It has been a good year for killing rubbish, and they are clean.

Winter-sown barley is coming on apace, but we have had to resort to the bird scarer once more to keep away sparrows. These seem cheekier than rooks; they return sooner after the bang, but not soon enough to do much damage before the next one. Sparrows are a major problem near housing estates, and are one reason for farmers removing hedges, as the little pests do not attack the middle of a field, only its perimeter.

The hybrid pullets are laying well, but pride of place goes to the yearlings just now. Their larger eggs command a higher price, and they are sustaining production remarkably well after being in lay for over a year. By all the rules they should go, but as long as they continue to leave a margin over feed costs they will be kept.

In August that year Philip Ward recorded one of his many sayings, but this time it worked against him. His corn bin gadgets are a reminder of the considerable amount of hand work still part of the everyday farming scene thirty years ago, as are his ideas for mechanized bale handling, now completely achieved from the tractor seat.

We were able to get into the winter barley at Chestnut Farm a week ago, and it is a good thing we did. More heavy rain a day or two later would have damaged an already laid crop, grown through in places, and the straw is still too wet to handle. The 6 acre field is part of a trial comparing spring with winter varieties. Weighed in bulk over the village weighbridge, the yield of eight quarters per acre disappointed me but allowance must be made for some loss through lodging. Spring barleys are still not fit.

'A man makes only one good second crop of hay in his lifetime', I was once told. If the long-range weather forecast is accurate, this will not be the year, and rather than waste time spoiling a crop in the field, ours will be regretfully ploughed in.

Record potatoes have been dusted against blight, and roots generally look well.

During the pre-harvest period we have fitted two perforated metal sheets, set on bricks, to the floor of one of the circular grain silos. The holes do not go straight through, each having a hood over, and this farmer-invented idea means that the fan which dries the corn may be used to empty the bottom of the silo. It avoids the dusty and unhealthy job of shovelling out that part of the bin not cleared by gravity.

Man-handling bales from a large acreage of straw has become a problem. It is slow, and there is risk of bodily injury from constant lifting of 4 stone packages. We have two ideas. One is to buy a grab attached to the fore-end loader, which will then lift a pile of six or eight bales. The snag is having a one-purpose machine, a thing to avoid if possible.

A bale elevator fitted to the trailer would mean that the tractor driver, and one man loading, could do the job. Bale heaps set close together would bring forty or so bales within range at each stop, and the tractor driver would set bales on the elevator, instead of forking aloft. Many bale handlers look attractive enough under demonstration conditions, but snags develop under the pressure of field work.

Our year-old hens are still laying on rations based on 'tail' barley, plus protein, and wheat and maize for high energy. A block of 108 hand-operated battery cages may be bought second-hand quite cheaply, and by cleaning once and feeding twice weekly, little time is needed to bring in a small regular income. On farms without a milk cheque, this is very welcome.

In September Philip Ward was conscious of the need to control wicks, wickens or couch grass, on his lighter land where the rhizomes spread rapidly. Part of Chestnut Farm was heavier; Philip always referred to it as 'bodied land'. In September came a reminder that the heavy-duty sacks so long an essential part of the farming scene were disappearing, as they were at High Wolds Farm (page 8). Today, no one would even contemplate slashing a hedge by hand.

Stubble cultivations are under way, using the rotavator whenever it is too wet for harvesting. We have trouble with 'wicks' on the lighter land, and must keep close watch for any rapid increase. It will pay us to spray one field at least.

King Edward potatoes are taking up well – a good, clean sample, and a second dusting against blight had the desired result.

Another wet-day job has been to sort and dispose of 600 12 stone sacks. We have no need for them after installing bulk grain handling, and farmers still using sacks are glad to pay 1s or 1s 4d apiece, instead of hiring.

Bulk handling of grain does mean that yields are difficult to assess. In the old days there was a certain satisfaction in counting the notches scratched on threshing machine sides by tough men, who boasted of their prowess at carrying 16 stone 'up steps'. Now that the self-emptying silo is working 100 per cent, corn is not man-handled between field and store.

Despite miserable harvest weather, we have managed to combine half our cereals on this arable farm. Straw disposal is a problem these days, and we feel lucky in having sold straight from the field so far. It has gone direct onto wagons, saving us a lot of work, and the baler is keeping fairly well up to the combine.

A bale collector, which dumps loads in eights or tens, has proved a useful and cheap acquisition, being marketed at reduced price after use at demonstrations. Skilfully handled, it will tip loads in straight lines, so that two men can stack in the field in very little time. Then along comes the wagon with elevator attached, and 5½ tons of straw may be loaded in only three moves. All these little points do count.

I have always been concerned about the batteries of a combine which stand idle for eleven months of the year. It is all very well saying they should be properly maintained – this job just doesn't get done. Instead, batteries have been hired for harvest at 7s or 8s weekly, saving both on capital and depreciation.

Pullets continue to lay well, and egg size is satisfactory, price increase again helping.

A contractor's mechanical hedge trimmer has been at work on the field cleared of Pioneer winter barley, and in two hours over 450 yd were neatly finished. All we do is clear up the trimmings. With a skilful operator, the standard of work is good, and the output many times that of the most energetic hand slasher.

Tradition and modernity mingled in Philip Ward's philosophy. He derived obvious pleasure in working his land in the time-honoured and well-proven way, yet stressed the countryman's role in encouraging both game and wildlife.

Whether to sell corn now in store, or to hold on, will depend on our merchant's advice. We have had the same one for years, and they know far more about what is likely to happen than the rest of us.

A post-harvest job which has pleased us immensely is thorough cultivating and rotavating of stubbles; this should encourage any weeds to germinate.

On a shoot here a fortnight ago there were more partridges than for two or three years. A Lincolnshire friend confirmed this.

At our Harvest Festival we had an excellent sermon from a country vicar, stressing farming's place in conserving the countryside, and the value of little copses and ponds. In the next post came a leaflet from the Game Conservancy, making much the same points.

One abundant harvest has been the wonderful crop of conkers. It is delightful to think that boys are just as keen on this old game as we were, and our ancestors for many generations.

'The farmer's foot is the best manure' is again proved in March 1970. Observations on the colour of the soil in March 1970 were followed by action.

All farmers hope for an early spring, but at Chestnut Farm winter routine still holds sway. This arable farm is 200 acres, half light land and half stronger, over clay subsoil. Attention to drains is thus essential and has been the major occupation during this week. The farm carries no livestock other than battery hens and yarded bullocks in winter.

When my daughter, Charlotte, and I walked over Long Field the other day we noticed how the land was shaded lighter above the 3 in laterals, becoming gradually darker as we moved away from them. These drains were laid 22 yd apart and should draw 10 or 11 yd on either side. Evidently they are not functioning as they should, so we shall have to find out what is wrong. At this season we check the manholes and silt traps; this is not a big job, though an unpleasant and wet one.

The flail spreader made short work of deep litter poultry manure used on the root land. We obtained useful help from Ministry of Agriculture Bulletin No. 67, Farm Waste Disposal. It lists dispersal methods and application rates for liquid or solid manures.

Potato seed is a bit tricky this year. Reliable once-grown Redskin is difficult to come by, but fortunately we have sufficient of our own. Pentland Crown seed is scarce, as so many people have gone off Dell. One retail customer has asked for Record, and this we obtained from a neighbour.

The meeting on potato diseases previously mentioned was so successful that it will be repeated at another market town, Malton.

Our manual potato planter has had several years' service, so I have considered replacing it with an automatic one. This requires only two men, but unless seed is very even it may block or over-sow. I must avoid the temptation of changing to a new machine when the old one is almost as satisfactory and needs only one more man.

During ploughing we have had very large flocks of seagulls, but have not seen any redstarts. Judy, working in Guildford, reports seeing large flocks in the Surrey countryside. The beagles enlivened ours last week, providing a lot of fun without a kill. Sunshine and drying winds are what we all need now.

Field amalgamations have led to the loss of many ancient field names, but Philip Ward's concern for continuity caused him to keep them. Happily, several farmers, after changing numbers, have reverted to the old, practical system.

Field names remain an interesting feature of the northern countryside. Often they have been handed down for generations, and are usually descriptive of a natural feature. Chestnut Farm is among the majority where names are retained in preference to more prosaic numbers.

Corn sowing is well advanced. A neighbour began corn sowing on 28 February on light land and we followed soon afterwards. Sultan barley was drilled in Cemetery Field, with more Sultan on Pond Field's 10 acres. This was barley after barley, so the 4 cwt corn manure per acre was slightly more than given to Cemetery Field, where cereals follow potatoes.

Holly Bush, Ireland North and Becks are three strips from which dividing hedges were removed many years ago. This year they all happen to be in the same crop, so may be drilled lengthways. Normally, each must be drilled north to south, but their 25 acres total is certainly easier to work as one block.

Stackyard Field and Lucerne are to go in with sugar beet any time now. Monogerm seed is being used at 4 or 6 in spacings.

Potato prices are not very healthy; we still sell by direct sales licence, but sales to wholesalers have difficulty in realizing the guaranteed price of £16. Stocks may be offered to the Board, but this entails putting them up when required, which may be at a busy time.

I'm afraid that many Rabbit Clearance Societies will have to close. This is the result of withdrawal of grants, which cost just under half a million pounds annually. It seemed a reasonable way of keeping the pests down, for we certainly don't want to see rabbits back.

The local society has an excellent gamekeeper who is there all the year, and who also kept on top of the moles.

Three hares were gambolling about the other day, but if they become a nuisance they are easier to deal with. I also saw three cock pheasants walking round the edge of the stackyard as large as life. Their plumage was really magnificent in the morning sunshine.

In 1974 a dry spring was recorded, but Chestnut Farm's potatoes had got away well and were not suffering. Philip Ward was delighted by the progress his bullocks made at pasture, but sadly he was not to farm much longer.

Different crops reacted in different ways to the June drought. While early-sown beet looked well, the latest sown field was in need of a drink.

The way in which weather and politics affect the working of five northern farms is recorded weekly in *Farming Post*, and together they form a reliable farming barometer.

Sugar beet in Chicken Field was place-drilled at 8 in spacings and has just been hand-hoed. It is not as good as the crop in Becks Field, which in turn is not the best in the district, but may be as profitable as any because it has not been hand-hoed.

Barley and wheat were both well-established when the drought came, and spraying was completed soon after my last report five weeks ago. We have now done all we can until harvest, at which stage the 160 per cent of normal sunshine and 60 per cent of rain experienced a week ago would be welcome.

Despite the dry time, potatoes in Lucerne Field look particularly well. They completely cover the rows, in contrast with a neighbour's only a quarter mile away, which show a lot of bare earth. We chitted all our seed, and the fact that they had 2 in of growth when put in the ground gave them that extra start which enabled them to grow away.

The crop has been sprayed against weed, and is now clean and free from disease. It has four times the leaf area per tuber compared with a gappy crop, and so takes full advantage of morning dews.

The bullocks improved tremendously on going out to grass. They have certainly peeled off the pasture, but I hope they need not be sold until autumn. The four best were kept inside and are fat, but market prices are about half of last year's peak level, and feed costs have been enormous. For this reason few livestock men are able to buy fertilizer in advance, although they know it will pay them.

The village is holding a Summer Fair today. Our village hall needs renovating, and with events from children's country dancing to the final whist drive, we hope to make sufficient.

Philip Ward, pioneer contributor from Chestnut Farm.

LOW FIELDS FARM

From the pinnacle of the Ouse Bridge on the M62 near Goole a countryside of great fertility may be seen. Yet less than two centuries ago a similar vantage point would have looked southwards over a rather desolate waste of peat, with only a few sparse trees and shrubs to break the monotony.

Though not within sight of the bridge, Low Fields Farm, which took over the column from Chestnut Farm, lies a few miles inland beyond Goole Fields on Swinefleet Common. Drive through it just before harvest, and you pass the Barker family's 700 acres; field after field of heavy crops of oilseed rape, peas, sugar beet and potatoes, with many acres of winter-sown wheat.

The fertility of this flat land is among the highest in England. Yet despite its enormous potential, Alan Barker and his neighbouring farmers are always

The farmhouse view over level, stone-free fields.

aware that, at high tide, the River Ouse at Swinefleet runs above the level of their fields, and that eternal vigilance is needed to prevent reconquest by the sea. Down the ages there have been several examples of land won and lost, to be reclaimed only after enormous cost and effort.

Friars' Hagg and High Wolds Farm have both been improved by enclosing fields from uncultivated land, then fertilizing, stocking or ploughing to increase output. At Low Fields Farm the very soil itself is man-made, or at least diverted by man from elsewhere, and is quite different in character from the original. It is completely free of natural stone, a circumstance unimaginable to the Addisons of Friars' Hagg. It has a high lime content even when mixed with peat from below; its pH reading is 7 or over, against the neutral acid–alkaline figure of 6.5.

This has been achieved by warping. In *The Standard Cyclopedia of Agriculture* (1910), T. Hallissy of the Laboratory for the Investigation of Soils, Ireland, concisely explained the process:

> Warp is a deposit of silt laid down, chiefly at river estuaries, through the agency of a system of artificial irrigation or by natural flooding. In the districts of the Humber and its tributaries, the practice of warping is extensively followed in the reclamation and improvement of low-lying swamps, by means of which these wastes have been converted into arable land of high fertility. The method adopted consists essentially in diverting the mud-charged waters of these rivers, when they become dammed back by tidal currents, and leading them over the ground to be ameliorated. Here, by embankments and sluices, the waters are confined within a definite area until they have deposited their burden of silt; they are then run off, and the process is repeated as often as may be found necessary. Warping is obviously possible only when the lands in the neighbourhood of the rivers are below the level of high tide or flood.
>
> In Egypt the periodic inundations of the Nile similarly enrich the level tracts along the river. In the process of time these accumulations have converted arid land into one of the most fertile regions of the world.
>
> The soil produced by warping has all the characteristics of fine alluvium.

According to Marshall's *Rural Economy of Yorkshire* (1788) warping was first practised in Britain on the banks of the Humber, coincidentally by one Barker, a small farmer at Rawcliff, between 1730 and 1740. It was afterwards extended by Richard Jennings of Armin, near Howden, in 1743; but until about the year 1753 it was not attempted by any other person. That is an indication of how communications as well as road and rail transport have

This isolated building, known locally as the Castle, was an inn and a blacksmith's shop. It is host to a pair of barn owls.

altered the countryside. Through *Farming Post* and the agricultural press, a similar innovation today would be known about by most farmers within the year.

Louden in 1883 stated 'the season for warping begins in the month of July, and continues during the summer'. The lands then become 'the soonest dry', and the tides 'are less mixed with fresh water, in which condition they are constantly found the most effectual'.

None of this would have been possible without the work of Cornelius Vermuyden, brought over from Holland in 1626 by Charles I with instructions to drain the whole of Hadfield Chase. His was the guiding hand behind drainage schemes covering vast areas of the Fens, including establishment of the Dutch River in 1635, which enabled water levels to be lowered before it joined the Don. Beside it in Old Goole stands The Vermuyden public house, only recently closed. Seven public houses in Goole provided accommodation for the Irish labourers who dug the early drains, and one long road is still called Dutchman's Mile.

The Romans used the Trent and the Ouse to ferry food from the grain-growing Fenlands of East Anglia to their garrison at York (Eboracum). Viking raiders found that the wide rivers gave them easy access to inland areas. They settled at this important river junction, and the many villages ending in 'thorpe' indicate their presence. A local chieftain, Siwardbar, rebelled against William the Conqueror's invasion, and joined Hereward the Wake at Ely. The nearby villages of Fockerby and Ablingfleet both appear in Domesday Book.

In 1821 the Swinefleet Warping Drain was begun. It is over 3 miles long, and took three to four years to complete. The Drain cost £18,000 in the pre-grants era; private capital provided it all. The Land Drainage Act, which enabled landowners to carry on drainage work using loans from public funds, was not passed until 1846. Warping from the Swinefleet Drain began c. 1830 and was finished c. 1840.

Depth of warp at Low Fields Farm varies from 0.5 to 1.25 m. That depth has remained constant in the century and a half since it was deposited from the river, unlike the peat, which continues to shrink as it dries. The drains from which the warp flowed were naturally drawn straight, and the field boundaries follow them. Thus the roads servicing these fields are also straight, quite unlike the winding tree-clad English lanes that inspire poetry.

Every dyke maintained by the Swinefleet and Reedness Drainage Commission has a number, and each farm pays a Drainage Rate of up to £7 per acre in some areas. Chairmen of the many Internal Drainage Boards have very responsible positions.

'Drainage is a very emotive subject here,' says Alan Barker. 'Modern pumping techniques have brought great improvements, but they must be organized and financed, with the threat of extra high tides and storms from the sea always in mind.' During his father's tenancy, good drainage of the area was achieved through installation of a pump in the early 1970s, combined with widening and deepening the main drains. The depth gained enabled all fields to be drained into this main.

The Axholme Joint Railway was built between 1900 and 1904, and cost £400,000. It was the main link with markets for the thousands of tons of arable products, for the roads even just after the Second World War were still very primitive. In 1926 4,000 tons of peas and 7,500 bundles of celery went by rail to Epworth in three days. It was said that if the bridge over Swinefleet Drain was bombed, Lancashire would starve. Two hundred of Low Fields Farm's 500 acres were given over to potatoes during the Second World War, whereas the safe period between crops to control eel worm is four or preferably five years. Even today a chemical deterrent is used.

The tree roots were a constant frustration. They appeared to rise upwards, and a field could seem clear of them only for a fresh 'crop' to show the next year. In fact they were a product of improved drainage, for as the peat dried it

Malcolm Barker beside a dump for roots which appear near the surface as the peat shrinks following drainage. Low Fields Farm has yielded many hundreds over the years.

shrank, which left the stumps emerging. The farm staff became experts in removing these obstructions, a constant menace to machinery, and spent hours and days on the job. The roots still appear, but much less frequently.

The Barker family had for several generations dealt with difficult land and set-backs. Alan Barker's grandfather farmed 80 acres at Bretton, near Wakefield, West Riding, with a pair of horses. That is now classed Grade III land, and in the depth of the depression in 1927 his son Horace persuaded him to move to Edderthorpe's 450 acres of Grade II land between Barnsley and Doncaster. In 1948 Alan and his brothers Maurice and David persuaded their father, Horace Barker, to take a still bigger acreage of Grade I land, the family's present holding.

Good staff relations play a constant part at Low Fields Farm. More men are employed here than on any other of 'The Year Round' farms, while three sons work at home or in the family partnership. In the very first diary from this arable holding in 1976, reference is made to arranging as many staff holidays in June as is practical. That is one of the few slack periods, before pea-vining starts. Then comes corn harvest, followed by potato and sugar beet lifting and all the rush of autumn cultivations. In June there is also a good chance of fine weather for the staff and their families.

The other main holiday season is over Christmas and New Year, which again suits both parties. Staff can enjoy themselves at late night parties without the need to rise early next morning. Work on the land is seldom urgent then; loads of sugar beet and potatoes may be on order, but the farmer and his family can usually cope. They also feed the livestock, though that side is now complicated by 16,000 laying birds, whose eggs must be collected and washed daily.

The attitude of 'putting the farm first' rubbed off onto the diminishing number of casual workers employed. In the early days, Irishmen helped with the potato harvest at Low Fields, and their struggles in wet conditions are recorded in November 1976.

Low Fields Farm comprises 585 acres of South Yorkshire warp land, won in years gone by through controlled flooding of the River Ouse. As tenant here and as a member of a 2,250 acre family partnership, I farm land without a single natural stone in it.

The cropping is 125 acres of vining peas, 225 acres of winter wheat, 67 of barley and 67 of potatoes, with sugar beet on 58 acres. Small acreages of Brussels sprouts, strawberries and tulip bulbs complete the cropping, the balance being one paddock and roads. The only stock carried are sixty to seventy head of barley beef cattle, a few geese, and a pony.

Spraying 75 acres of late-sown peas has been our most recent job, and hoeing between the rows of Brussels sprouts is finished although I have a real tale of woe to tell about this crop. Grown here for only the third time, it has been reasonably successful until this year, when a plague of hares attacked the young plants. I had to dash off to a Hull grower and buy plants, which were put in with a neighbour's transplanter. Only 1½ acres of the original 5 acres escaped damage, and drought has added to the problems.

Nor has it all been plain sailing among the sugar beet. Millipedes attacked 6 or 7 acres of the crop, eating through the pelleted seed, and the whole area had to be treated. On the other part, spraying against the aphids that bring virus yellows is being done.

One of our eight tractors is fitted with the sprayer at the start of the season, and it is not removed until the spraying is finished. Similarly tractors set to various wheel settings are not altered. All this is to save time, as our activities are purely commercial.

A strong point is made of arranging as many staff holidays as possible in June. Work on pea-vining begins early next month and four regular full-time men are employed on this, in addition to my son, one school-leaver, and a farm fitter and lorry driver who serve the estate.

In that year, corn harvest finished very early, on 12 August. The date revived memories of another early harvest; family farms can always associate the season of the year with some event of special significance.

In 1959 we finished harvest in Low Fields Farm on 20 August. That was the day our daughter was born, so it has remained firmly in memory and never did we expect to achieve an earlier finish. This year combining was finished on 12 August, though we could not say that all was safely gathered in as some bales remained outside.

The harvest was so early and easy that it made us impatient. The winter wheat should have been given an extra few days, but the combines were poised for action and we pressed on. This proved a mistake in view of the apparently endless fine weather.

Old farmers round here say 'Never pray for rain on warp land', but the potato ridges are very dry. The best drought resister here is variety Pentland Crown, which will yield 10 or 11 tons an acre, followed by Pentland Squire and Stormont Enterprise. I was foolish enough to risk twice-grown seed with the Desiree variety, and I am paying for it with some virus disease. The potato haulms are dying back, but as there is probably still a few hundredweight to the acre of growth in the crop, we are reluctant to start lifting.

Ever since these stubbles were cleared, two sets of drags and one of disc harrows have been working steadily. Thus the autumn cultivations have been almost completed, and two of the drivers asked if they could take a week's holiday, knowing we were almost worked up. This is typical of the thoughtful attitude of our staff, and it will give them a rest before potato lifting starts.

Every available building was filled with straw, and 80 acres were sold in the field. The new John Deere 975 combine went through harvest without a hitch of any sort, unlike the pea viner which was in constant trouble.

A burnt-out corn elevator motor caused a frantic hunt round the countryside for a replacement, and in the day and a half that it was out of use, tractor scoops had to do the job. A mobile seed-cleaning plant dressed 24 tons of Huntsman, 5 tons of Maris Fundin, 4 tons of Mega, and 6 tons of Maris Templar. The proportions represent the way these varieties of wheat performed in the 1976 harvest.

By November, the good progress had been almost completely nullified, and the familiar story of a wet autumn on low-lying land unfolded.

It is a tale of woe from Low Fields Farm this month. Of our 66 acres of potatoes just over two-thirds have been gathered, but a great many have been

'Drainage is an emotive word here,' said Alan Barker. Without these carefully maintained dykes, culverts, pumps and under-drainage the whole area would revert to bog.

left in the ground. The land is so wet on this sea-level Humberside warp that, in the worst places, 4 or 5 tons an acre remain.

I doubt whether we shall be able to harrow them to the surface later; a great change in the soil will be needed. Some terrible ruts are left by tractors and trailers, and despite picking by hand behind the old-fashioned spinner with its deflector removed, we simply cannot avoid the loss.

The farm road to the potato field is so bad that drivers take a load of stone on each return journey, to fill the worst holes. The potatoes have bulked wonderfully since the rain started, and the Pentland Crown variety is yielding 12 tons an acre, despite those wasted.

All our ploughing is done with a crawler tractor and a one-way plough. Our output is 8 to 10 acres a day, and this job is well advanced.

To overcome the difficulty of drilling winter wheat on very wet land, we hired a contractor's machine that blows fertilizer out of nozzles like a sprayer. With a 40 ft boom, we drilled 63 acres in one day, following behind with the crawler and spring-tined harrow.

Two men work away at the sugar beet, one driving the self-propelled harvester, and the other leading off. Less than 20 acres of the original 57 are left, but it is a slow job.

In parts, the beet have grown very big following the rains, and the flail that should simply sweep off the tops knocks these big beet out of line. If set

Motors housed above these troughs operate screws or augers which lift water from the dyke. This is done automatically when the water rises. The pear-shaped probe hanging between the troughs activates the second auger when the water reaches it. The original 5 mile warping drain receives the surplus, discharging it through sluice doors into the river at low tide.

higher the flail misses the normal stand altogether, so one man has to lift these large ones by hand.

Our Irish workers are very philosophical about the wet land. I saw one man knock his basket three times on the trailer side, and it still had six potatoes stuck in. There is 2 in of solid mud by the time the baskets have been filled many times, and the men each carry a little stick for scraping them out. If potatoes were not fetching a good price, it would not be worth the trouble.

In November 1982 the potato harvest was finished, despite a set-back through harvester breakdown. Here we meet farming's insoluble dilemma: heavy yields that bring low prices in their train, and an end result of much extra handling for less money.

October ended with a fine week at Low Fields Farm, with sugar beet harvesting going well ahead. Timeliness is all-important, for once the weather becomes really wet we are held up for a long period.

The potato crop is our most important and lifting finished three weeks ago. The last few acres were a struggle, for the rubber web on our harvester gave endless trouble. A replacement costs £1,250, a sum we wished to avoid paying before next autumn. In the event we had to give in and spend not only the money but three days in stripping and re-assembling the sub-frame before becoming operational again. This set us back after a splendid start, when for several days over 5 acres a day were harvested by one machine.

Variety King Edward was particularly pleasing, and yields generally very good. However, the price is so low that we are handling a considerable extra tonnage only to be worse off financially than with last year's moderate crop.

Trouble also occurred with the French sugar beet harvester. It had a topper in front of the tractor, while behind were lifters to put the six topped rows into one windrow, later elevated into a trailer. Spare parts became so difficult and expensive that we have abandoned the system and now use a single-row lifter that fills a hopper, which then tips into a trailer.

Winter wheat went in very well, but the 5 acres of Brussels sprouts are nothing but a headache. So many sprouts are bursting or spongy that there is the greatest difficulty in getting a clean sample, and I wish we had never grown them.

Entries in January 1984 confirm that 'the farmer's foot [or in this case the farmer's hand] is the best manure'. The tailpiece shows Alan Barker keeping in daily touch with his most important commodity.

Low Fields Farm is a very quiet place, with farmworkers taking a fortnight's holiday at about Christmas.

Most farms are purely arable, and spring, summer and autumn are very busy, with fewer and fewer men. A lot of holiday time in summer would embarrass the already crowded schedule, and fortunately the present arrangements suit all parties. Farmworkers now have three weeks' paid holidays, with people who have given long service getting more.

The only work to be done is foddering the fifty-two head of cattle, and even that is more a point of interest than a chore.

My sons and I have graded some potatoes, including a load of King Edwards, for which we gained a £2 per ton premium.

A supermarket chain gained publicity two years ago by decrying the variety Pentland Crown, and refusing to stock them. At the time I said that with good management, including a heavy seedrate to encourage medium size tubers, a nicely matured Pentland Crown was as good as any. Now we have gained £5 per ton premium from the same supermarket for Crowns.

I peel the kitchen potatoes myself, so always know what the quality really is.

Power harrow followed by clod separator.

Cooperation between family and staff is again underlined in May 1986, keeping machinery going round the clock.

Potato planting at Low Fields Farm started on 1 May. On that hectic day we also put in one drilling of peas on rented land, and sprayed all 50 acres of sugar beet.

The next day staff concentrated on potato planting, using the two-row machine. We covered 18 to 20 acres, our best ever, as past work was limited by the power harrow's 1 acre per hour output. This time one son harrowed till 2 a.m., and another driver took over at 5 a.m., so the planter could go nonstop.

On the Saturday the drill wheels, tool bar and drawbar were stolen from the roadside. This could only have been for scrap; they would fit no other machine, and it was more a nuisance than anything. Then we all worked right through Bank Holiday weekend to catch up with planting, for last year all potatoes were in by 19 April.

Corn spraying has been a real problem. Usually it was either too windy or too wet, and one of my sons pressed into this task had to snatch opportunities, working late into the evenings as the wind dropped, as long as he could see the 'tramlines' or undrilled working rows.

Wheat has been delivered by our own transport to the Gunness wharfe, which lies 15 miles away on the Trent. Best achievement was 124 tons in one day. The dairy heifers went out to grass on 16 May, grazing four little paddocks here, and a rented canal bank.

In 1987 the dead time of year is enlivened by the arrival of more unusual birds, while extra work in the holiday season was rewarded by a bonus on potato prices.

January has not been a particularly productive month at Low Fields Farm. Staff took a fortnight's holiday over Christmas, and then most of another week when snow made access difficult.

Despite all precautions during the very nasty spell of cold weather, we still had frozen pipes when the cattle pulled the lagging off.

We still managed to riddle 170 tons of potatoes in a fortnight, being rewarded by a premium of £12 to £15 a ton as we could guarantee that tubers were frost-free, and made some efforts to open the farm road.

The 120 by 30 ft lean-to on the potato store is completely insulated, enabling us to work in comfort, and store the sorted crop safely until the lorry arrives.

Though winter wheats have survived the snow very well, oilseed rape is patchy and a bit disappointing. We have few woods near, so pigeons are not the pest they are elsewhere. The only land work scheduled is to spray a few headlands against grass weeds.

My friends say I am paranoid about pea prices, but the fact remains that returns are depressing, and we shall have to make up our minds whether to sow a proportion of the pea acreage with spring barley.

My wife picked up an interesting bird in the goose pen. It was a water rail, which according to the warden had probably travelled 5 miles inland along the dykes from the reserve. We also had a greylag goose on the lawn.

Another occasion when finances did not work out right was in May 1989. After a flurry of effort to clear the old potato crop, the farm was left with none to sell, and . . .
'The best-laid schemes o' mice and men.
Gang aft a-gley.'
Mice are listed as one of the farm pests, their more usual role being among stored grain. In the days of finger-bar grass reapers, field mice built their round nests at just the height in the grass where the cutter bar's fingers impaled them, bringing an abrupt halt to proceedings and a flurry of wrath on the innocent creatures.

Skylarks also caused a nuisance, but as a bird-watcher the farmer just shrugged his shoulders. Here he talks about a 'chain' as a unit of length. He does not follow tradition for tradition's sake, realizing rather that 22 yd is a sensible length in which to count the number of plants, and from it estimate the plant population per acre.

For once we managed to sell all the old-crop potatoes at Low Fields Farm before planting the new ones. The last load went on Friday 14 April and we began setting the 1989 crop on the following Monday.

We congratulated ourselves on our valiant efforts, until the lorry driver returned with our empty boxes. 'Why aren't you sending any more?' he asked. 'The price keeps going up!' Anyway the first field of potatoes is just through, showing 40 per cent emergence. We used a clod separator, which lifts clods and stones from the growth area and deposits them behind the rows. Not that we have any natural stone on these below-sea-level Humberside acres; clods and soil sticking to the potatoes are our problem.

Potato planting finished on Tuesday 2 May after working and paying overtime all holiday weekend. Then it was so fine for the rest of the week that we could have had a weekend off after all.

The clod separator ensures a fine tilth for the potato crop. Hard clods could affect the bloom and shape desired by supermarkets.

sugar beet drilling ended on 31 March. We daren't make too fine a seed-bed, for this warpland runs together if it rains and forms a crust that affects germination.

But mice favour the looser tilth and run along a row and dig in exactly over the seed. Skylarks have also attacked one row, nipping the first two cotyledons from about a chain.

In 1991 swedes were grown for the first time for many years. They were for human rather than stock consumption. In May they showed erratic germination, in marked contrast to the sugar beet with its desirable plant count per chain. The swedes eventually did well, but grew to such a size that mechanical harvesting proved difficult. They became a target for jests from neighbours. The root harvester's progress ranged from dead stop to very slow and, as this flat warpland yields few hiding places, all could note (and comment on) the slowness of gathering the swedes.

sugar beet at Low Fields Farm is germinating well compared with last year. I counted eighty-five plants to the chain, the ideal number being seventy-two to seventy-five.

In contrast, newly drilled swedes are showing erratic germination. This is the first swede crop for many years and is destined for the factory that takes

Free-range poultry have ample chance for exercise. Note the pop-hole on the building side.

our peas. The swedes will be diced and frozen, and we accepted the contract because the EC cannot tamper with it.

Heifers for my son's dairy farm are out to grass. Before they went, one was blown up, and died after I fed them. We await the knackerman's verdict.

Generally the farm has never looked better though there is a bit of scorch on some cereals following late application of liquid nitrogen and straw shortener.

One potato field is covered with oilseed rape seedlings, although it is seven years since that crop was grown there. We hope to spray them off before the potatoes emerge.

Our egg buyers threaten penalties if we are late in accepting their birds, but offer no compensation when our production is held up by them.

We are considering some form of stand-by generator for our two free-range poultry houses at Low Fields Farm. Though not as essential as with a controlled environment, power is needed to operate the belts conveying eggs to the packing shed. When the present flock is replaced in February, the older system in our first house may be scrapped, and the roll-away automatic one installed.

Inside the egg packing room. Eggs arrive here by conveyor from the automatic nests.

After two dry summers, peat under the metre of built-up warp has shrunk, so buried tree stumps give the impression of working upwards. In thirty years we have dug out literally hundreds, yet they still occur to damage implements. Our tractor driver had to replace four shear-bolts when ploughing just once across a large field. I bought the last dozen bolts from our dealer, who has sold 1,000 this season.

The saga of our swede harvest continues. We have abandoned mechanical lifting for the time being, as in one gappy area the swedes weigh up to 2 stones each and the machine cannot take them. This sounds a typical farmer's exaggeration story but the tractor wheels nudge the big swedes so that the harvester does not accept them squarely and chops off too much.

Ten acres of wheat remain to be sown on sugar beet land, this year's main wheat varieties being Riband, Beaver and Haven.

A flurry of activity resulted in automatic nest boxes being fitted in the nick of time before the next birds arrived. Both sugar beet and swede crops are coming through nicely.

Potato planting is finished at Low Fields Farm, though not without set-backs. We broke a shaft on the potato planter and one on the clod separator. Though we have no stones on this Humberside warpland, rough clods can affect the sample, and the separator lifts and deposits them between the rows of plants, to be further crushed by the tractor wheels.

The new batch of poultry for one free-range house arrived yesterday. We were only just ready for them, as work was complicated by installing automatic nest boxes.

The sugar beet has emerged as well as it ever has. That drilled before the rains shows eighty plants to the chain, with seventy-five from later drillings, which means almost 100 per cent germination.

Swedes are showing 75 to 80 per cent emergence. The second field will be drilled on May Day, as last year.

Wheats and peas look well, though 200 acres of the latter need spraying against pea weevil.

Wheat prices have fallen slightly, but any remaining stocks were sold forward. The last two loads of potatoes similarly made less money.

Beef and dairy heifers are now out to grass.

A year later the beet was showing through equally satisfactorily, and Alan Barker showed no signs of relinquishing his opinion of the old English chain as a useful unit of measure in modern farming.

John Barker does most of the spraying. The self-propelled machine was designed and built in Norfolk by Neil Sands. It has wide low-ground-pressure winter tyres and an 80 ft boom. The storage tank in the background was installed in 1948 for fuel for the grass drying plant, used for ten years. Grass was grown in an attempt to get rid of potato eel worm.

Although this Humberside warpland is among the most fertile in Britain, there is an annual worry about sugar beet. Clay content is such that 'capping' of the soil surface may occur if rain is followed by wind and sun. It is like baking a brick, and the tiny seedlings cannot force through. This year's showery weather has been ideal, resulting in full germination and over eighty plants to the chain. Some years there have only been forty plants to the chain of 22 yd, a measurement we still find the most useful whatever EC might think of it.

The spring cropping looks surprisingly well, with the first flowers on the peas, but wet and windy weather has upset our spray programme. The only fine day coincided with a farm walk.

Another spraying job that went wrong could not be anticipated. We use a pre-emergence spray on the swedes, but the crop came through in a record five days after drilling, and we dare not spray. We have resorted to expensive hand hoeing, and good hoers are scarce.

Birds from the free range poultry houses go out next Monday. It is a messy, sweaty job that no one likes, but our staff just get on with it.

Three bullocks on a barley diet blew up and one died, while others on identical rations were unaffected. We are feeding stock-feed potatoes to try and salvage something from that crop.

Many a farmer knew exactly how the Barkers felt when other people's fields were humming with harvest machinery, and they decided that theirs was not fit. Inspectors calling at short or no notice did not help.

We still have 8 acres of wheat to harvest at Low Fields Farm, after a dreadful ten days with over 3 in of rain. Before that we did manage to borrow two extra combine harvesters from the family, doing 30 acres in one day.

We had a very uneasy time in late August, with combines working all around us, while we waited for our corn to dry. This paid off, as the bulk of the wheat was harvested at 15 to 17.5 per cent moisture, although the last lot topped 25 per cent.

The combine has been fitted with a sophisticated and expensive grain measuring monitor. It gives output in tons per hour and yield in tons per hectare, and checks over a weighbridge showed it was 99.5 per cent accurate.

Alan Barker with beef calves bred on his son Simon's dairy farm.

It enables us to tell on the spot which varieties and treatments do best. It has also proved that our best looking crop failed to reach 4 tons per acre, whereas several other fields topped that figure. We expected that variety Riband would be top yielder, whereas Haven excelled it.

Our trial potato digs were a bit disappointing. The Desiree lacked size, and the King Edwards were so big that they had lifted the row in dry weather, and let in enough light to cause greening.

I'm disturbed by the Ministry of Agriculture attitude to inspections. Northallerton office phoned at 6.00 p.m. to say they were coming to check ear numbers on seventy cattle at 9.00 a.m. next day. It would have been impossible had we been harvesting. Free range poultry inspections show similar disregard for vital farm operations.

A new if very expensive potato harvester proved a real boon in November 1993's very sticky conditions. Alan Barker was particularly delighted that it was British made.

Frost was welcome at Low Fields Farm. This low-lying Humberside warp land is very wet and sticky after the autumn rains, and the sugar beet harvester can

Filling the potato planter at Low Fields Farm.

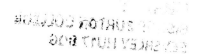

travel for only a few hours each morning before the frost goes. Last weekend we had 20 acres remaining, and rate is only about 3 acres a day. We always reckon to finish beet before Smithfield Show, starting tomorrow, a week earlier than usual.

Then the land must go in with winter wheat if not too late. The seed is here, and October-sown crops look well. Our staff has loyally worked weekends ever since mid-summer to keep pace.

A noticeable feature has been the absence of wind. Some years we are absolutely fed up with constant buffetings across these flat acres, but our tree-fringed lawn was deep in leaves for weeks.

Litter in the free range poultry houses is unsatisfactory, in spite of being changed. Price of wheat is down below £100 a ton, and I'm glad the merchant persuaded me to sell wheat forward, and keep the oilseed rape, now strengthening.

Potato lifting ended on 18 October, and last month's mention of our new Scottish harvester brought requests to hire. Sadly we were unable to comply, as the manufacturers bought it back with an unbeatable offer.

I watched a short-eared owl fly up from a main drain, and later saw a small flock of tree sparrows, easily identified by chestnut heads and black cheek spots.

The potato planter in action.